Meditation without Gurus

A Guide to the Heart of Practice

Clark Strand

Walking Together, Finding the Way
SKYLIGHT PATHS Publishing
Woodstock, Vermont

Meditation
without
Gurus

Meditation without Gurus:

A Guide to the Heart of Practice

2003 First SkyLight Paths Publishing Edition

SkyLight Paths Publishing is creating a place where people of different spiritual traditions come together for challenge and inspiration, a place where we can help each other understand the mystery that lies at the heart of our existence.

SkyLight Paths sees both believers and seekers as a community that increasingly transcends traditional boundaries of religion and denomination—people wanting to learn from each other, *walking together, finding the way.*

Library of Congress Cataloging-in-Publication Data
Strand, Clark, 1957–
[Wooden bowl]
Meditation without gurus : a guide to the heart of practice /
Clark Strand.—1st SkyLight Paths Pub. ed.
p. cm.
Originally published: The wooden bowl. 1st ed. New York :
Hyperion, c1998.
ISBN 1-893361-93-4 (pbk.)
1. Meditation. I. Title.
BL627 .S757 2003
204'.35—dc22

2003013895
10   9   8   7   6   5   4   3   2   1
Manufactured in the United States
SkyLight Paths, "Walking Together, Finding the Way" and
colophon are trademarks of LongHill Partners, Inc., registered in
the U.S. Patent and Trademark Office.

Walking Together, Finding the Way
Published by SkyLight Paths Publishing
A Division of LongHill Partners, Inc.
Sunset Farm Offices, Route 4, P.O. Box 237
Woodstock, VT 05091
Tel: (802) 457-4000   Fax: (802) 457-4004
www.skylightpaths.com

for Deh Chun

Acknowledgments

Literally hundreds of people over the years, many in chance encounters, provided the inspiration for this book. Some, like the cab driver who told me he wanted to meditate but didn't want to wear a turban, reminded me of who I was and what I ought to be writing about, even when both of these seemed forgotten.

My wife, Perdita Finn, formed this, as all else that I write, from the base metal of my daily musings. Whatever gold lies herein, the reader must attribute to her alchemy. Likewise, my mother, Anne Strand, provided valuable insights about the overall conception of the book. My daughter, Sophie, provided the inspiration for several chapters—besides which, she is the most playful and alive person I know—and my son, Jonah, just by sitting in my lap while I wrote some mornings, simplified my thoughts.

As always, Ned Leavitt and Kip Kotzen kept my writer's life on keel. And Laurie Abkemeier at Hyperion made everything clear.

Finally, I am grateful to my Zen teacher, Eido Tai Shimano Roshi, Abbot of Dai Bosatsu Zendo, Kongo-ji, for his guidance over the fourteen years of our association. This book could not have been written but for him. Likewise, I wish to express my thanks to Marvin Sicherman for his help in finding what was lost.

Contents

Introduction

The path forward seems to go back.

Tao Te Ching

One morning during the fall of my sophomore year in college, I woke to find that, quite unexpectedly, the bottom had dropped out of my life. Had I been a careful observer of myself, I might have seen it coming. My friends were not surprised. That morning I went to the dean's office and informed him that I was leaving.

"Can't you just talk to the counselor?" he asked.

For the first time in months, I laughed. "What I'm feeling isn't depression," I told him, "it's despair."

The next day found me seated on a bus for upstate New York, where I had been told there was a Buddhist monastery where I might find a Zen master who could help me find some meaning for my life. At that time I had not yet discovered that, against all probability, there was a Chinese Zen master living just six miles from my dormitory in a little two-room shack.

Ten years later, following a marriage ruined by neglect and spiritual *dis-ease*, I found myself a Zen Buddhist monk in

charge of a New York City temple where people came to
meditate twice a day. I had a shaved head, an impressive set
of robes, and was next in line to succeed my teacher, the
temple's abbot. But when I looked in the mirror, I no longer
recognized the person that I saw. All I had wanted in the
first place was to find the simple truth about who we are
and how we ought to live. Instead, I had found another job,
a different set of clothes.

I wanted to leave, but I had promised the abbot that I
would remain in charge during his sabbatical in Japan. So,
for another year, I continued to oversee the usual daily
meditations and silent weekend retreats. But I no longer
meditated in the way I had been taught. Instead, I asked
myself one question: Was there a way for people to slow
down and experience themselves, their lives, and other people in the present moment without adopting a new religious or philosophical ideology? Could meditation exist
outside of an ideological framework in a way that was
merely human but nonetheless profound? What would happen if that experience, so long confined inside the various
boxes of the world's religions, were instead set free?

When I finally sat down to write this book, years after
becoming a Buddhist monk, and even years after abandon-
ing the Buddhist monkhood, I first had to ask myself what
good there was in writing a book at all. There were so many
books on meditation already, and the truth was, I couldn't
help but think that Americans might get closer to meditation if only they put all those books in a pile and burned
them. But that seemed unlikely.

The only choice left was to write a book of my own and be sure to include a set of matches, hoping the fad might catch on, and that by burning this book readers might feel inspired to toss a few others on the fire. In that way we could come back to what we have always known to be most true: that being present to nature, to oneself, and to other people is the only life there is.

This is a book that shows you how to meditate all by yourself, but it works even better if you can do it with a group. It doesn't require that you have a teacher or that you travel anywhere special. It isn't particularly complicated. You aren't likely to forget how it's done, and if someone asks you what you are doing, after reading this book you should be able to explain it to them very easily. In fact, after hearing your explanation, they may even want to try it themselves. The only thing it requires is that you be willing to remain a beginner, that you forgo achieving any expert status, that you treat meditation as a kind of hobby, not as a neurotic preoccupation or a job. In other words, it requires you to maintain a spirit of lightness and friendliness with regard to what you are doing. It's nothing special, but it works.

PART 1

Getting Started

Teaching Is Impossible

"Meditation cannot be taught." So said my first teacher, Deh Chun, an elderly Chinese hermit who lived the last years of his life in Monteagle, Tennessee. "Only learning is possible," he said, "*some*times."

What he meant was that meditation can only be practiced. If it is taught, then, by definition, what is taught is not really meditation at all, but something else. Some method or philosophy, but not meditation itself.

When I consider the years of our association, the most remarkable thing is that I cannot recall any particular thing I learned from him. I can't point to a particular conversation we had and say, "Well, you know, then Deh Chun said such and such and everything was clear." At the time, *nothing* was clear. When I think back on it now, I realize that his entire teaching consisted of being in the present moment, with nothing else whatsoever added on.

Being with Deh Chun was like dropping through a

3

hole in everything that the world said was important—education, progress, money, sex, prestige. It was like discovering that nothing else mattered and all I needed was *now*—the moment—to survive. Sitting there in the little house, listening to the water boil, to the twigs crackling in the wood stove, I was temporarily removed from the game. That was the genius of his teaching, that he could bring forth that transformation without even saying a word.

His was a state of complete simplicity. Like water, the direction of his life was downward, always seeking lower ground. When I met him he lived in a ramshackle two-room house heated by a wood stove the size of a typewriter. There was no furniture, only a few turned-over crates and several cardboard boxes in which he kept his clothes. His bed consisted of two sawhorses on top of which he had placed   a three-by-five sheet of plywood and a piece of packing foam. I remember thinking once that this bed suited him perfectly, his body was so light and small.

A similar structure in the other room served as a desk for writing letters and for painting his ink-wash Chinese landscapes. Propped against the back door were spades, a shovel, and a rake, tools he used to tend a plot of land the size of two king-size beds laid end to end. With the exception of tea, soybeans, peanut butter, molasses, and occasional wheat-flour, whatever he ate came from there.

We would sit in his little house without saying much of anything. Early on I learned that he was not disposed to give instruction in any formal way. He would serve me lunch, or sometimes breakfast if I'd managed to get there early enough, and then I'd wash up. Afterward, we would talk about his garden, or more likely we would remain silent for a long while and then it would be time to leave.

Nowadays, in books on meditation, it has become standard practice to say that your teacher was a mirror that allowed you to see your true self. But that was not my experience with Deh Chun. It was more like floating weightless on the Dead Sea and looking up at an empty sky. There was a feeling of tremendous peace and freedom, but that was all. I didn't know *anything* after I was done. Trying to pin him down on some aspect of meditation was as pointless as trying to drive a stake through the air. He taught one thing and one thing only, and that he taught to perfection: meditation happens now.

After the first few visits to his house, I realized nothing pivotal was going to happen, but I kept returning anyway without knowing what it was about him that held my attention. I was a college student, and fairly typical of other nineteen-year-olds in that I was not particularly interested in spending time with someone four times my age. Especially someone who by ordinary standards was little better than a bum.

Deh Chun was completely simple. He lived on fifty dollars a month. He was a Buddhist monk who never spoke of Buddhism, an accomplished landscape painter who never sold his work. He wore only secondhand clothes and was without pretension of any kind.

Long after his death, it is finally clear to me that he taught only by example. Recently, a friend of mine said of a certain Catholic priest, "He practices what he preaches, so he doesn't have to preach so loud." Deh Chun practiced so well he didn't have to preach at all.

Meditate as a Hobby, Not as a Career

Think for a moment about your hobby, if you have one. If you don't, think about the thing in life that you most love to do. How much time do you spend each week gardening? How much time knitting or playing golf? How much would you *like* to spend?

Before he retired, my wife's father was a surgeon. But, as my wife always says, he was a surgeon so that he could sail. So that he could live on the water and take long vacations every year on the ocean. "Thinking back on it," she says, "he was always happiest scraping barnacles off the boat."

You don't expect to get anything out of a hobby but the thing itself. You engage in a hobby because you enjoy it or because it relaxes you. You don't become frustrated because you should have done it better, or because you missed a day. In fact, the whole idea of a hobby is to let go and experience something for itself, for the satisfaction and pleasure you take simply from doing it. You don't do it for your self-esteem, for the world, or for inner peace. Your relationship to it is simple, natural, and not self-conscious at all. If it were self-conscious, it wouldn't give you so much pleasure. It wouldn't be a hobby anymore.

Like a hobby, meditation ought to be a time when you can occupy your mind with something for its own sake, without getting caught up in any of your usual preoccupations: Am I doing this right? Are the others doing it better? I'll probably fail at this, just like everything else. It ought to be an area of your life where you can let go of the obsessive desire to improve yourself, to get ahead, or to do better than anybody else. And yet, without realizing it, this is exactly what many meditators do.

Some feel neurotically driven to achieve a higher level of self-esteem, as if to meditate were synonymous with "being good." Others meditate for psychological health or for a lower pulse rate. Still others for better karma or a more exalted spiritual state. They go off for long retreats to find themselves, leaving their families behind. But where are they going to find themselves if not in the lives they have?

Meditating as a hobby is actually a far more honest approach to meditation than treating it like an obligation, a moral responsibility, or a job. When people tell me they are meditating for peace or to improve the world, I always think they don't yet know what meditation is about. Not that meditating doesn't make us more peaceful or give us a generally more positive outlook on the world, but that it is impossible to meditate with such a goal in mind. I am always more impressed when people tell me they meditate because they like it, or because their lives are so busy that once a day, for a few minutes at least, they just want to have some peace of mind. In my opinion, this is a lighter, more open approach. Ultimately, it is also more direct.

Once meditation rises above the level of play its possibilities are diminished. Why? Because when meditation loses its lightness it becomes like everything else—another object of desire. When we meditate for something other than meditating, we only become further ensnared in the endless cycle of getting and spending, whereby every activity in every moment has to have a goal. Reaching that goal yields fulfillment or happiness, failing brings disappointment or despair. To treat meditation in this way is not only ineffective, it actually makes matters worse, because then there really is no hope for peace or happiness, fulfillment or love, because these things, when they happen, always come from within us, and always happen now.

Meditation ought to decrease the drivenness of our lives, not make it worse. That is why I say meditate for its own sake, as a hobby, without losing the lightness of your first approach. That is why I say don't become an expert, but stay a beginner instead. Because if you treat meditation as a career, then it becomes concerned with achievement. And when that happens meditation becomes fundamentally no different from the desire to get ahead, to get more money, or a better job.

The person who meditates—whether for five minutes or five hours a day—wants to keep one area of his or her life that is not driven, that does not draw them ceaselessly away from the fundamental *enoughness, sanity,* and *beauty* of the world. The person who truly meditates, and is not caught up in some neurotic game, knows that peace, love, happiness, contentment—everything happens now.

Practice

Begin by closing this book and just sitting quietly where you are for a few minutes. Remain still and do not speak. In fact, don't do anything at all. One teacher calls this "facing the blank stage of your mind."

Once you have done that for a while—say, five to ten minutes at most—you will probably want to open this book again and read more about meditation. But please pause for a moment before you do that. Rest assured that there is nothing you will read herein that was not implicit in your first experience of meditation. Even knowing nothing. Even not knowing what to do.

If you are not a beginner and are coming to this book after years of meditation practice, or if you have already read many other books on meditation, try for a moment to forget everything you know and just start over. Try your best at becoming a beginner again.

Begin now.

An Evening Talk

I recently began a talk by saying, "Please take a moment to be present." Then I waited for a few moments before going on. Doubtless, my listeners must have thought this was some kind of preliminary—a way of getting everyone focused before going on. Instead, it was the entire text of the lecture. After that, I got everybody talking, explaining to one another what they had done during that brief interval of time.

One woman had uncrossed her legs, putting both feet flat upon the floor. Another relaxed her shoulders and took a deep breath. One man took a breath and held it. Many others closed their eyes. Some meditated. And a few listened to the sounds around them in the room.

The point was, virtually no one in an audience of sixty or seventy people had just remained the way they were. Nobody felt present to begin with. Virtually everyone felt they had to *do* something to be present instead.

Meditation is not something we *get*. It is not something that comes to us as the result of effort over time, but rather something that we have to begin with, if only we can summon enough clarity to see it. To meditate is to return to our natural state, the condition of wakeful simplicity that exists when distractions have fallen away.

In the morning I meditate briefly before starting to write. After sitting down and taking a few deep breaths, I straighten my spine, relax my shoulders, and begin to count my breaths from one to four, simply noting each outbreath at the moment it occurs and saying the number silently below my breath. Nearly always, there are some stray thoughts that intervene, and I have to cut these thoughts and start over several times. After a few minutes though, I settle in. I begin to feel present where I am.

Once this happens, I stop counting and begin to *follow* the breath instead, noting the physical sensations of each inhalation and exhalation at the moment they occur and riding those impressions somewhat in the manner of a down feather floating on the wind. Eventually the feather becomes lighter, more like a single dandelion seed, until finally it disappears altogether and there is only wind. When I have reached that point, I forget about following and start to meditate without props or images of any kind.

At that point, nothing further needs to be done, because I am no longer distracted—not by thoughts, not by worries, not by other people, or by the world. And yet, paradoxically, I am more with myself, more with other people, and with the world than ever before, because I am finally really present. Right here. Right now. There is no other time.

Start with Nothing

Twelve years ago my friend Anita flew to Washington, D.C., to spend the weekend with her brother, Paul. No sooner had she arrived at the airport than Paul announced that they were going to attend a one-day retreat at a local meditation center. "It'll be good for you," he said. Anita had never meditated before and let her brother know that. "It doesn't matter," he replied.

"We were late, it was raining, there was no time for preparation, no time to think," Anita told me. "We stopped at a Burger King and Paul handed me this little paperback book on meditation and said, 'Here, read this chapter on Mind.' Needless to say, I couldn't take any of it in."

Because they arrived late, she wasn't told what to do with her posture, her attention, or her breath. Soon everyone gathered in a room with fifteen or twenty cushions and simply sat still upon the floor.

"So what did you do?" I asked her.

She thought for a minute and said finally, "I think I spent hours just looking at the floor."

It sounds like a funny thing to say, but nowadays few of us are lucky enough to have this kind of experience the first time we meditate. On our first visit to a meditation center, we are far more likely to be given a routine set of instructions. Such instructions, while they have the advantage of giving us a clear sense of what we are supposed to *do* in meditation, have the disadvantage of leading us to believe that we can meditate by *doing* something. In fact, for most of us, meditation involves *not doing* what we normally do.

The more defined and precise the initial set of instructions on how to meditate, the less likely it is that one will have the authentic experience of meditation the first time out. This is a shame, because there is always the possibility of beginner's luck, even in meditation—and perhaps *especially* therein.

By now you have already meditated for the first time, if only for five minutes, or even for just a second or two. Perhaps you noticed a few things. For instance, when all of its busyness is taken away, the body usually begins to get restless. It doesn't know what to do with itself when it is perfectly still. The same thing happens when all of the props are pulled away from the mind. We are so used to doing one thing after another all day long, from the time when we get up in the morning, until the time we close our eyes to sleep at night, that we seldom have the experience of a pause, a moment when we are not doing anything at all.

For most of us, our chief orientation in life is this more or less continuous stream of mental and physical activity. When that becomes disrupted, we may get brief glimpses of a freer, more spacious world. Or, if our lives are particularly driven, we may feel momentarily disoriented or even fearful. We all have experiences like this from time to time. But life, especially modern life, almost seems designed to diminish their importance, their potential to enrich and nourish our lives. Sometimes it happens that a person's life is changed by such a moment, by the sudden realization that he or she is somehow more or greater than what they think. But more often it happens that at such moments, we say to ourselves, "Better get on with it, I've got more important things to do."

To allow these pauses to occur is *meditation.* To widen them and allow them to flower in your life is the *practice* of meditation, a practice we can do alone or with other people as part of a present moment group.

But what is inside of those pauses? How are we supposed to identify them? How are we supposed to know if we are meditating or not? The answer is that they are simply pauses—brief discontinuities in the fabric of our mind. They have no fixed content, and in a very real sense, when we experience them directly we have the momentary sensation that there is nothing there. That is why I say that, even though we will now go on to learn about such methods as *counting* and *following* the breath, it is best to start with nothing. That way, even if you become confused about something later on, at least you will know at bottom what meditation really is.

Practice

Begin by sitting down in a comfortable upright position. No need to worry yourself just now over the details of posture; we'll get to that later on. For now, just breathe naturally in and out through your nose. Take a moment to notice the breath at the moment it comes into your body, and then again at the moment it goes out.

Now that you have noticed the act of breathing, close this book and try counting the breath for two or three minutes, just to see how it feels. Count from one to four, one number for each exhalation, coming back to one when you have reached four, or whenever you become distracted and lose count. Only count the outbreaths. Let your mind relax briefly while you are breathing in.

Begin now.

Counting the Breath

If nothing else, our initial experience of meditation usually teaches us one thing: it is difficult to sit still and do nothing. In fact, we often get confused just trying to imagine how we ought to approach such a thing. For this reason, it is best to begin each session of meditation by counting the breath. Breath counting calms and clarifies the mind. It is the perfect vessel in which to cross the stormy seas that rage inside our minds and bodies in the midst of a busy day. After a few minutes of focusing ourselves in this way, we find it less difficult to concentrate. The body and mind are brought together under one common enterprise. Thus it becomes easier just to be where we are.

The Thai meditation teacher Ajahn Chah once observed, "There are people who are born and die and never once are aware of the breath going in and out of their body. That's how far away they live from themselves." If you have never noticed the breath before now, just in its own

right, just for itself, then you have now crossed an important threshold. You are no longer one of those persons
about whom Ajahn Chah spoke.

Noticing the breath is the point of entry into the world
of meditation. This is true, to differing degrees, in almost
every spiritual tradition around the world. There is evi-
dence of this connection even in such commonly used
words as *spirit* and *inspiration*, both of which derive from
the Latin word *spiritus*, meaning "breath."

By focusing on the breath, by staying with it from one
moment to the next, we bring the body and mind together
in one place, at one time, which is the present. But how do
we keep them there? Given the fact that in life, distraction
is not the exception but the rule, how do we keep our minds
focused on something as simple as the breath?

This is where counting comes in.

You probably noticed that it was easier to meditate by
counting the breaths than it was by doing nothing.
Counting the breath gave you something to focus on—and
also something to come back to when your mind became
distracted and you lost the count.

Perhaps you were able to count the breaths easily for
one or two minutes without once becoming distracted and
forgetting to count. In any case, as you continue to do this
practice you will find that, although it is sometimes easy
and other times nearly impossible, counting is always the
right place to start.

Later we will learn about following the breath and,
finally, about meditating without methods of any kind.
Even then, however, you will want to begin here each time

you meditate, just as you enter a house by walking through the door. Breath counting is a way to remind yourself to settle down and be present. It is a way of reminding yourself to take life simply, one moment at a time.

Coming Back to
Where You Are

To begin with, we meditate by allowing ourselves to do just one very simple thing, and that is to count each outbreath from one to four, returning to one at the end of every cycle, or whenever our minds wander and we lose count. This is all you have to remember to begin meditating. It is the foundation for all that follows.

If you can do it.

The fact is, once we begin to calm and clarify the mind in this way, we discover an important truth: Our minds are so scattered, so often distracted by thoughts and worries, or by random impulses like "Oops! I better call Mother," that it is almost impossible to do anything in a direct and simple way. So, ironically, the first lesson of meditation is always failure, and in some ways that is the most important lesson of all.

Once we have failed several times to count our breaths from one to four, we begin to realize how much we really need to meditate. We begin to get some understanding of the moment to moment quality of our mind. We begin to notice more readily, for instance, when we feel overexcited, distracted, or tired. This may not seem like much, but the truth is that we are often out of touch with our emotions or our state of mind.

This awareness of how easily distracted we are—of how unstable the quality and content of our mind is—becomes the foundation for our practice of meditation. So it is unnecessary to perform meditation perfectly on the first try. It is far better to build a strong foundation for our practice by discovering our actual state of mind. Consequently, when you meditate, it is important not to berate yourself for failure. Failure is merely the moment your awareness sharpens and you return to "one."

This is a difficult lesson. We are all so goal-oriented, so conditioned by society to regard every new undertaking in terms of success or failure. Though the "goal" of breath counting is to count the breath from one to four without losing count, frequently the most vivid awareness actually occurs at the moment when we realize our minds have wandered and we renew our effort by returning to "one."

It may seem like nothing at first, this coming back to "one" whenever your mind wanders and you fail to count the breath. But something is happening after all. You are breaking the pattern of habitual thinking which, up until now, has ruled your life. Simply by refocusing on the breath and coming back to one, you are demonstrating for yourself that you are the master of your own body and mind.

This is nothing esoteric. You can watch the way it works each time you meditate. Then, gradually, your moment by moment state of mind will become lighter and more friendly. You may even find that it is less difficult to live a happy and productive life. More and more, you will come to see that many of the worries in your life are self-imposed, and that much of the general unsatisfactoriness of the world is the result of not really being *with* it and *in* it, here and now. Once this happens you will realize that meditation, which at first seemed so difficult, is really as simple as coming back to where you are.

The Proper Way
to Breathe

Examine your breathing right now as you are reading this book. Is it shallow? Deep? Is it slow or fast? Whatever your answer, that is the proper way to breathe.

I don't mean to suggest that you will always want to breathe this way when you meditate, but rather that there is no right or wrong way to breathe. The object is to count the breath, not manipulate it. If you manipulate your breath, as you do for instance in certain kinds of yoga, you may very well develop an altered state of mind. If you breathe very fast and shallow, you will quickly begin to feel lightheaded or overexcited; if very slow and deep, then your thoughts may slow to a crawl. However, neither of these states has anything to do with meditation.

Most people get caught in the idea that meditation is (or should be) quiescent—very soft and steady, like a cruise ship crossing a tranquil sea. And of course if that happens naturally, it's fine. But you are likely to get yourself in trouble if you try to induce such a state, because then you have to spend a lot of time cultivating the physical and mental technology for creating and maintaining that kind of condition. Even if you achieve this, it isn't going to help you much unless you plan to become a Himalayan hermit. (I hear they wall themselves up in a cave, leaving only a small hole to put a plate through. The local people feed them for years while they do nothing but meditate.)

The important thing to remember is that the breath is alive. For that reason it changes from one moment to the next. As well it should: imagine having to breathe slowly and deeply while you are running. If that happened you wouldn't be able to run very far. So don't get caught up in any yogic notion of what constitutes the proper way to breathe. If you are a believer in one of the Eastern philosophies which says that the proper circulation of *chi* (breath energy) is the secret to health and happiness, fine. Just don't do it when you meditate. Give that practice its due, but at another time.

Having said all that, you will probably notice that once your mind and body have settled down, your breathing will become smoother and more relaxed. Chances are, it will slow down perceptibly and it may sometimes feel deeper as well. This is a good sign, but it isn't something you should aim for. As golf pro Harvey Penick said in his *Little Red Book*, "Whatever you do, do not try to relax." Trying to relax and breathe deeply *as an act of will* distorts your breathing as much as it does your golf swing. It's much better just to take the proper position and prepare your mind and body for meditation by counting the breaths from one to four.

Where to Place Your Attention

When you meditate it is natural to want someplace to focus your attention. Because most meditation teachers like to keep such random aspects of meditation tightly sewn, they almost always tell their students where to put it. The sad truth is, however, that wherever you put it, your attention will wander all about. At some time or another it will want or need to be someplace else. I recommend letting the attention settle wherever it wants. That way you won't lose your concentration if it decides to take up residence in some other part of your body.

However, I ought to mention what can happen if you let the attention become too fixated on one particular spot. If it becomes arrested on the spot between the eyebrows, you may get a headache or experience dizziness; if right below the navel, you may begin to feel so settled in that spot, so overcome with a sense of stability and well-being, that very soon you may become obstinate or even aggressive; if it is arrested at the crown of the head, you will begin to feel transcendent. None of these feelings has much to do with meditation, however. They simply induce certain states of mind in which you are likely to get stuck. Meditation isn't about getting stuck in any particular state of mind. Meditation doesn't get stuck anywhere. That's the whole point.

To help you keep from getting stuck in some particular mental or physical state, it is a good idea to keep the eyes half open when you meditate. If you focus your eyes on a general area a few feet in front of you on the floor, you will find that it is easier to keep your balance and sobriety. With the eyes open, you are less likely to fall asleep or to daydream—and less likely to lose touch with reality.

A Word about Posture

Up until now I have said nothing about posture, which many people consider to be the secret of meditation. There is a reason for that.

Posture is a place where many people get stuck when they first start to meditate. As important as it is to keep an upright spine, it isn't worth losing your head over. And it certainly isn't the single determining factor in whether you can meditate or not. I know of one famous Zen master who was never able to straighten his spine fully because of an injury sustained as a child. Consequently, his head always tilted a few inches to one side. He used to tell his students who had difficulty meditating, "If I can do it, so can you."

My first formal meditation teacher only gave me one word of instruction in the whole first year. "Sit," was all he said. Had I taken up residence in the Zen monastery where he lived, I would certainly have been offered more.

But as circumstance would have it, I left for home right away, carrying all my enthusiasms wrapped neatly around that single word.

Of course, I had no idea how to do it. But I had a few books on meditation in my personal library, and all of these seemed to agree that sitting in the full lotus posture (legs crossed, with each foot resting on the opposite thigh) was the best way to go, so that was the way I forced myself to sit.

Forced is the right word. My body didn't want to do it, but by stretching for ten minutes before each session of meditation I was able slowly to work my legs into something approaching the posture of a buddha, until finally I was able to sit that way for twenty minutes.

But I cried the whole time, it was so painful. And instead of counting the breaths from one to ten, as they do in the Zen Buddhist tradition, I counted from one to one hundred, which I discovered took approximately twenty minutes to perform. That was the only way I could endure the pain.

A few years later, when I attended my first retreat at the monastery, I could sit in the full lotus posture for forty minutes at a time. Without crying. But there was no way I could sit that way for forty-minute session after forty-minute session. Not all day long. Not for seven days.

By the third day I had lost all the feeling on the tops of my big toes (it never came back) and had realized that I could never last until the seventh day. At that point I told my teacher that if I were to continue the retreat I would need to be allowed to sit in a chair. "I was wondering how long it would take you to realize that perfect posture is not the point," he said. "This is not charm school after all."

For our purposes, any position in which you can meditate comfortably for fifteen or twenty minutes at a time is generally okay. The perennial meditator's wisdom suggests a posture in which your back is straight, your shoulders relaxed, and your head not turned or tilted to either side.

The hands should be held in such a way that they are not a problem. Usually that means with the palms turned upward resting in your lap. Or you may rest them facing downwards on your thighs or knees.

The main point is to keep the back straight but relaxed. With a straight back everything about meditation is made easier. The breath flows more smoothly. You are less likely to feel uncomfortable or fatigued. And it is easier to stay alert. All in all, sitting with a straight spine just *feels* better.

When the Japanese master Dogen came back from studying Zen in China, someone asked him, "What did you get?" Dogen answered, "Eyes horizontal, nose vertical." This statement could be interpreted literally as "I got good posture." Or "I got my head on straight." Still another interpretation would be, "I learned to be upright and honest in all my dealings with the world." Dogen's statement probably means that the secret of meditation is just sitting down with the body vertically aligned.

Elsewhere I have said that you ought not to get too obsessed with any of the details of your meditation practice. But that is not the same as saying that the details are unimportant. Just don't become obsessed with them. "Eyes horizontal, nose vertical." Keep it just that simple and everything else will follow.

Body and Mind

Take a few minutes to consider the correct posture for meditation. By now it should be clear that keeping your back straight is the main thing. But what exactly does that mean?

Consider the shape of the back. In most people, the back curves inward slightly just above the buttocks, before swelling out again toward the middle of the back. It then curves back toward the front again when it reaches the neck. In anatomy, this is what is called a normal curve.

Most of us have backs like this, but certainly not all. Some suffer from medical conditions like osteoporosis or scoliosis. Others, perhaps those who have spent long years in the army or at ballet, will have lost some of this normal curve over the course of their training. Still others may have lost the lower (lumbar) curve from sitting at an office desk eight hours every weekday for twenty or thirty years. So it would not be advisable for us to conclude that there is one posture for meditation that is right for everyone.

When we say that you should sit with a straight back when you meditate, we don't mean straight as measured by a yardstick. Take a second to look at your own body. How many straight lines do you see? Not many. As you learn to meditate, you will discover that a straight back is not measured by a ruler, but by your state of mind.

When your shoulders are slumped forward, your lungs become compressed and your circulation works less efficiently. After sitting like this for a few minutes you are likely to become fatigued. If your chin falls forward toward your chest, you will soon begin to daydream—or maybe even fall asleep. If your head is tilted to one side you will feel off balance, and if your body leans too far forward or backwards, you will have to tense your muscles to stay upright. After doing this for five or ten minutes, those muscles will start to burn.

You will know that you have a straight back when these impediments to meditation have disappeared. Unless you sit inside a hall of mirrors, or have somebody take photographs of you, that is the only way you will know for sure.

The best way to develop good posture for meditating, therefore, is to watch your state of mind very carefully as it relates to the position of your body. If sitting in a certain way—for instance, using a Japanese *seiza* (kneeling) bench—takes the strain off your muscles and makes you feel more alert, then sit that way. If you are sitting in a cross-legged position like the half lotus, in which one foot is placed resting on top of the opposite thigh, try placing just the edge of a meditation cushion under your buttocks.

This will lower your knees to the floor, enabling you to assume a more stable posture. But check this out for yourself.

It may be that your legs are too stiff or too muscular to sit cross-legged. In that case, sitting on a meditation cushion may feel a little like trying to stay balanced on top of a basketball. In that case, you'd better try using a chair. By placing a small cushion on the chair at the back of your buttocks, you can achieve the same feeling of stability and support.

The key point to remember in finding the correct posture for meditation is ... correct for *whom?* If you are trying to imitate some posture you have seen illustrated in a book on meditation, you are going to have a problem right away, because every aspect of meditation, including something as seemingly objective and observable as the posture, is entirely subjective. Always, you have to find your own way. So keep that spirit of inquiry and you will soon discover what manner of getting seated works for you. At a certain point, the body and mind just click together and become one thing, here and now. When that happens, you will have found what sitting with a straight spine means for you.

Practice

Take a seat right now in one of the postures for meditation: either in a chair, sitting cross-legged, or kneeling on the floor. In any of these positions you may need a cushion or bench or some other device to put under your buttocks in order to keep your lower back from caving in. If you need it, find a cushion now before we begin.

Once you are seated, take a deep breath and let it out all at once through your mouth. This is a way of letting go of many of the accumulated tensions of the day. Next, relax your shoulders and place your hands either in your lap, with the palms overlapping, facing upwards, or on your thighs or knees, with the palms facing down.

Rock your upper body gently from side to side, first in larger, then in smaller and smaller arcs, until finally it comes to rest in an upright position, perpendicular to the floor. If you need an image to help you visualize this process, think of a compass needle swinging back and forth until it finally points north.

Do you feel stable in this position? If so, let the eyes come to rest on an area of the floor a few feet in front of you. Is your head tilted or turned slightly to one side? If so, gently bring it back in line.

Once you have found the correct posture, relax a little—not so much that your body loses its alignment, but enough so that you can breathe naturally.

Now you are ready to begin. In truth, by taking this posture, you have *already* begun. But we'll talk about that later.

Begin now.

Where to Meditate

Only when I had left the monastery and returned to the life of a wage-earner did it occur to me that for years my meditation practice had been exactly like one of those little *bonsai* trees, an exotic specimen, raised under carefully controlled conditions, and pruned in accordance with the aesthetic of an exacting spiritual discipline, but essentially an indoor miniature that could not survive in the open as an ordinary tree.

To use a more modern metaphor, meditation takes place under laboratory conditions. There is no escaping this. Meditation begins as a self-conscious act, perhaps the most self-conscious act possible, since it involves watching one's own mind. The problem with this situation is the same problem encountered by quantum physicists when they try to observe subatomic particles: observing them changes them. It makes them behave differently.

In the same way, the conditions we set up for meditation determine, to a large extent, how limited, or how useful, it will be. The quantum physicist would have no problem if the world were a laboratory. In the same way, the monastic would be able to function perfectly in the real world if it were run by monastery rules. After years of temple life, I had to start over from scratch upon entering the busyness of the outside world.

Where you meditate has everything to do with how useful your meditation will be. But by where, I don't necessarily mean in which room of the house, or whether you live in a quiet spot or not. I simply mean that you should meditate inside the life you have. If you are an accountant, meditate inside an accountant's life. If you are a policeman, meditate inside of that. Wherever you want to illuminate your life, meditate precisely in that spot.

The Myth of Silence

Maintain a quiet atmosphere for meditation, but don't get the idea that quietness and meditation are the same. If you do, you will not be able to meditate when your stomach growls. And if someone else is restless you may feel angry and disturbed. Real quietness doesn't work that way.

I once saw a television special that consisted of interviews with Nobel Laureates in physics. Most of the interviews took place in what appeared to be professors' offices. But there was one interview, with an Indian physicist, that was conducted at his home. This, it turned out, was where he actually did his work.

In one segment, while the interviewer asked questions about quarks and black holes, the physicist's wife bustled about in the background making tea. In another, several children raced back and forth between him and the camera, knocking objects off his desk. Moreover, it was apparent that these were the conditions he worked under every day.

Once or twice, he seemed to wish the kids would go away, but he was nevertheless able to sustain a complex train of thought throughout the interview.

I found myself wondering if this particular man might have found the atmosphere of a university office stultifying, and maybe that was why he did his more creative work at home. The atmosphere was hardly sedate, but it seemed to work for him. Perhaps that was the place he felt most connected to his deepest thoughts.

What to Sit on

Every golf pro is familiar with the person who shows up on the course with two or three thousand dollars' worth of equipment, but who can hardly hit the ball. In the same way, having the right cushion, the right kind of incense, or a beautiful bell isn't going to make you meditate any better. Chances are, to start off with, you'll do better if you have fewer external distractions of this kind.

The only really essential thing is to have something comfortable to sit on. To begin with, you could just use a folded blanket from your bed. You can also use any of the devices traditionally used for this purpose—meditation cushions, Japanese *seiza* (kneeling) benches, a prayer rug—anything that helps you remain still for fifteen or twenty minutes at a time. The important thing is not to get fixated on the equipment of meditation.

My own teacher, Deh Chun, had none of these things. Each morning he simply sat upright in his bed, crossed his legs and meditated, without any formality whatsoever. The only ritual object I ever saw in his little house was an inexpensive statue of Kuan Yin, the Bodhisattva of Compassion. It was the color of bone and, like nearly every other thing in his little house, not entirely clean. Years later, when I was living in Manhattan, I saw one just like it in Chinatown. It was on a shelf in a stationery store along with twenty or thirty others. They sold for $5.95.

Practice

Stop now and take time to notice the breath for a moment before reading any further.

What did you do in order to notice it? Did you inhale deeply? Did you breathe in through your nose? Did you straighten your spine? Think for just a moment about what you actually did in those one or two seconds before you were able to locate the breath.

Chances are, whatever you did to notice it was unnecessary. The breath is always there. All that is required to find it is to look directly where it is—which is here and now, coming into and going out from your body even as you read these words. The trick—and I hesitate to call it that, because there is actually no trick to it at all—is to see directly what is there.

I once told my meditation teacher that I was having trouble finding my breath. He laughed so hard I thought he would fall off his cushion. He was right, of course. I had been breathing in and out even as we spoke.

Finding Your Keys

At one time or another probably all of us have had the experience of looking for something that we were already holding in our hand. In my case, it is usually the keys to my car. When that happens, there always comes a moment of maximum frustration, when I have looked everywhere and the keys are nowhere to be found. My body is tight, tense. I may want to blame somebody—my wife, for instance—for having misplaced them. Or maybe I just feel as if I am going to explode.

Right at that moment, I usually realize that I have been holding the keys all along. That moment of realization is like waking from a nightmare—the keys were never lost to begin with, they were right there in my hand.

Usually, we feel a little foolish when something like that happens, but a moment later we are involved in something else and the lesson is lost. It will happen again, probably not for a month or two. But eventually it will.

The same thing happens in meditation all the time, only we may spend days, weeks, months, even years, looking for the breath before we realize that it was there all along. The lesson of the present moment is that what we are looking for is *always* right there in our hand. It's *never* someplace else. We start from that point with every meditation: first, reminding ourselves that to be present is our only aim; second, reminding ourselves that we are present already whether we realize it or not; and, finally, settling ourselves down enough so that we can count the breath from one to four. So that we can appreciate what is already ours.

Beginner's Luck

When we sit down to meditate, we are present right away. But usually we don't even notice this. It slips by us before we can engage it with the mind. An instant later, we are caught up with the *thought* of being present, and the *actual* present seems far away. Why does it happen like this?

When we first sit down to meditate there is a kind of freshness, or openness to what is going to happen. We haven't started yet, haven't thought about exactly what to do. An instant later, however, the mind interposes some thought like, "Oh, yeah. I'd better meditate. I'd better start to concentrate. I'd better count my breaths from one to four." And, of course, that's true. There's no way around it if you're going to meditate.

The trick is to seize that instant and start to meditate right away without any intervening, self-conscious thought. Simply begin. No need to tell yourself to do so. No need to say, "Now I'm going to do it." Just do it instead.

Once you've tried this a few times, you will have become acquainted with a phenomenon, well-known among meditators, called "the watcher." The watcher wants to be in charge. It wants to take possession. It wants to be in control of everything. "Okay," it says, "now you're going to meditate. Let me show you. This is how." Then it monitors your progress to see whether you are doing it right or not. If it thinks you're doing well, it will reward you with a comment like, "That's good. You did all right today." If not, it might say, "No. You didn't do it like I said." If you begin meditating right away, however, then the watcher will have nothing to do.

Think of it as beginner's luck. We all have it, even if we've been meditating for many years. Always there is a part of ourselves that is unobstructed by self-conscious thoughts, a part that can do things simply, in a direct and present-minded way. Probably everyone has had some experience of it. Playing darts for the first time, you hit the bull's eye. Then everybody claps. With the next dart, you take your time, aiming carefully and taking a stance, and miss the board entirely. That is how it works.

The secret of meditation lies in understanding that we all have this inner steadiness and calm and we can access it right away, without obsessively monitoring or telling ourselves what to do. We all have beginner's luck, and we can use it every time.

The Autopilot

When I used to give instruction in meditation, every once in a while someone, invariably a beginner, would report that they were having great success at counting their breaths. "I almost never lose count," one would sometimes say. "It's just so easy."

In the same way that having a very hard time with meditation usually means that you have lost your lightness, having too easy a time of it usually means that you need to come back down to earth. Usually, it means that you aren't actually very invested in the counting and, consequently, it has become something that you can do automatically, with just a portion of your mind. When this happens, it is a sign that you have been meditating long enough to develop an "automatic pilot," a part of your awareness that meditates while you get on with something else.

A sure sign that the automatic pilot is at work is when you can think of other things without losing track of your breath. If you are really focused on the breath, this won't be possible. If you follow some discursive thought, you will immediately lose track and have to start over at one. When this happens to me, and it still does every now and then, I always remember Gladys.

When I had just started meditating, I happened to spend some time at a meditation center where, in retrospect, the teacher was very good. I was a beginner and was having a lot of trouble with everything: the schedule, the meditation, all the rituals of center life. All of these problems seemed more apparent when Gladys was around. Even though she had started at the same time as I had, Gladys did everything perfectly, without a single glitch. She sailed through every activity with the confidence of a natural. So I was shocked one day to find that she had left. When I asked the teacher about it, however, he said that he wasn't surprised. "She wasn't very engaged," he said. "Didn't you notice how easy everything was?"

Take Five

This is a popular expression in many work environments. It usually occurs when there is a general lapse in performance brought on by mental or physical fatigue. "Take five," the boss says, because he or she has suddenly run up against the law of diminishing returns. From here things will only go from bad to worse, so it's better just to take a break and start fresh again a few minutes later.

What do people do during that time? Some smoke a cigarette. Others step outside for a breath of fresh air or to stretch their legs for a minute. Each person naturally knows what they need during that five minutes to refresh themselves. That is not the problem.

The problem is that, where our inner lives are concerned, none of us has an objective, outside observer to tell us when we are getting tired or stale. There is no one to tell us "Take five" before we reach the snapping point. As a result, very often we push ourselves too far. By the time we realize that our minds are befuddled, that we are overcome by stress, it is because we have slipped somehow. We've ruined the drawing we were working on, or snapped at our daughter. At that moment, if we're lucky, we just stop to collect ourselves for a moment to regain our composure before going on.

If we are really honest with ourselves, most of us have to admit that many times, during such moments of stress, we only make matters worse. "I'll give up on drawing altogether," the artist tells herself, ripping the paper from the pad. "You never pick up after yourself," the mother tells her daughter. "What kind of person will ever want to live with you when you grow up?" Later, when we have calmed down a bit, we may realize that we made a mistake. Or we may become so self-defeated or so self-righteous that we only become more entrenched where we are. We may only persist in feeling bad.

Meditation helps us to recognize problems before they get out of hand. How? By definition, meditation is the art of "taking five," the art of freeing the mind and body from wherever they have gotten stuck, restoring their natural flexibility and vigor. Whatever else is going on in our lives on a particular day, fortuitous or tragic, happy or sad, meditation brings us back to the present, where all such considerations are truly beside the point. Where, as one meditation teacher once told me, things will either get better, get worse, or stay the same, and our only job is to watch them with lightness of heart, knowing that, whatever it is, "this too shall pass."

When we do this, we are less reactive, less at the

mercy of all the ups and downs in life. We have a clearer, more vibrant sense of ourselves, even though that "self" may be elusive or hard to define. When we are in the present moment, bad things are less frightening. And good things are less likely to send us soaring out into the stratosphere where equilibrium and sobriety are lost.

Self-Help Hell

In the current milieu, it seems to me that more than a few of us are caught in a kind of self-help hell. In the effort to improve, modify, discover, or even heal the self, we have become ensnared in a system of desire, the unacknowledged object of which is to affirm the very feelings of dissatisfaction it claims to address. In my opinion, it is far better to take oneself out of the game.

What would happen if a substantial number of people just decided to give up hope of self-improvement, self-development, even self-discovery, and forget the self instead? What if, for fifteen or twenty minutes a day, we were to exist in the present without desire for anything at all? Would that be possible? And if it were, what would be the result?

Meditation is about forgoing spiritual and/or self-help technology of any kind except for coming back to the present, which is where we already are. In truth, it is a kind of non-method. It doesn't require doing something, but rather not-doing what we ordinarily do.

At some point the mind chimes in, "But what will the world look like if I do nothing? Will it be different or not? Won't everything just stop happening? Won't I just fall apart?" The real answer to these questions is to see for yourself. But I can offer an example that may help you to conceptualize what it might feel like to be this way.

Think of a painful, negative state of mind such as envy, the desire for what belongs to another. That feeling, and the burning anguish that accompanies it, is centered around the self, specifically, around an impoverished feeling that what one has (or *is*) is not enough. That pain, that feeling of inadequacy, has no resonance, no depth or body, without reference to the self. In a sense, that pain "belongs" to the self, and the self to it. In fact, that pain is both created and maintained by all the complex, interrelated ideas that we maintain about the self.

Once we understand this, it is easy enough to see that any method that seeks to address the problems of the self by "helping" the self, as, for instance, by building self-esteem, will ultimately not work. That is, while it may improve our level of functioning, it will never remove us from the game altogether, once and for all. In fact, the whole notion of self-help is basically a contradiction, only we can't see it because we fail to grasp the big picture.

What exactly is the "big picture," and how do we see it? The big picture is what emerges in the absence of a self-centered view of the world. We come to see it, not by addressing the self, with all its myriad problems, but by forgetting it altogether, by being present right now, as we really are. In this way, finally, we are able to see through the whole process—to see through the whole game by realizing that it *is* a game.

The way to see through this game is simply to cease all the routine maintenance, repair, and upkeep we normally do on the self from one moment to the next. Simply let things go. And how exactly do we do *this?* By doing nothing. By breathing and counting from one to four, and finally not even that.

Too Easy!

Soen Nakagawa Roshi once said of meditation, "Too easy! Too easy!" What he meant was that, most often, we overshoot the mark. We say to ourselves, "Now I will *really* meditate. Now I will *really* be aware." We tense our bodies. We grow very still. If, momentarily, our minds wander, we wrench them back. No wonder it doesn't work.

In reality, we only need to relax and stop fretting. But, of course, we all know how difficult that can be. Personally, I hate it more than anything when someone says to me, "Just relax for a second. It'll be okay." Even so, it is nearly always the best advice.

The problem is that, by the time someone tells me to relax, I have already reached the point of frenzy: to get somewhere on time, to fix the fax machine, to recalculate a large sum that doesn't figure—it doesn't matter what. Whatever it is I am trying to accomplish at that moment, I have become my own biggest obstacle. But how difficult it is to realize that I am the very thing that needs to get out of my way.

I am reminded of an auto mechanic I once worked for when I was in high school. When he got exasperated because some part he was working on wouldn't fit, he would shout, "Just stand *back*. Get out of my way." He said this regardless of where I was standing. I even heard him shout it when I was out of the well. Sometimes even when I was outside on the island pumping gas. I never had the nerve to tell him to just relax and take a breath. But I was young, and he was young, and for all I know he eventually learned it anyway.

You don't have to meditate to learn this lesson. Some people learn just by threading a needle. When you thread a needle, the natural inclination is to tense the body, to hold it very rigid and still, because the needle is so small and the thread so delicate that even breathing too hard may throw you off.

After you have failed two or three times to get the thread to go through, you will probably take a deep breath to dispel the tension in your body before going on. This is a natural reaction, a kind of safety mechanism executed by the body when it has become overloaded by stress. Often, after this happens, the thread immediately goes through.

If you don't use a needle and thread regularly, the lesson isn't likely to take. If you are a seamstress or a tailor, however, you are likely to have learned it long ago. But even a tailor isn't likely to apply this lesson to everyday life. To do that, we have to meditate. We have to get in the habit of watching our own mind. Only then are we likely to notice when we ourselves are the very thing that needs to get out of our way.

1917

One day, while looking through the 1917 diary of my wife's English grandmother, I realized that virtually everyone has some experience of the present in their lives, some area where they are content to relate simply and directly to the thing itself, whatever that thing might be.

Every day of her life Nellie Havens recorded the weather and the names of any visitors who came to call. If she went out for some reason, she also noted that fact. Typical entries:

Monday, March 26: Cold. Nothing in particular.

Tuesday, March 27: Showery. Went up to see Aunt Mary. Drews came after dinner.

Wednesday, March 28: Fine. Gardened. Evening class.

The entries are all fragments. There are few complete sentences, and even when anything of real historical significance came to her attention, it was spliced in between ordinary observations about the day.

> Saturday, July 7: Lovely. Office. Air raid about 10:30. Saw aeroplanes & shrapnel bursting in the sky from office window. Aunt Mary to lunch & tea. Gardened at Whitegate.

Not once in the diary is there anything of a decidedly personal nature. Why?

Some might say that Nellie's diary only reflects the impoverished emotional and intellectual life forced by circumstances upon English women of her day. Had she been a man, her diary would doubtless have been filled with more interesting, more important things. She would have been more likely to take an interest in the great events of the time. In any case, some others will say that, had she not been a member of the leisure class, she would have found little time to dwell on trifles.

While these observations may in part be true, I don't believe they tell the whole story. When I asked my wife about her grandmother—whether there had been anything unusual or remarkable about her—she said, "Later on, she was actually quite crazy. But she was supposed to be a great gardener. She could make anything grow." Once I heard that, I instantly understood.

Every day Nellie Havens wrote in a little book what the weather was. Rarely were these descriptions more than a single word, and many days she wrote nothing more than that. And yet, there is such a clear sense of the pleasure she took from writing it. She never missed a day.

Clearly, this was the place where her experience of life was the simplest, the least cluttered, and, paradoxically, perhaps the most profound. No wonder she was such a great gardener. Her connection to the weather was a clean, true line.

For others, perhaps, the same thing happens playing golf. In fact, it is no surprise to me that there are so many books nowadays touting the spiritual aspects of golf. When people are playing golf, they are actually more relaxed, more receptive to spiritual truths, than when they are out to *get* them. Their relationship to golf is direct and simple, not troubled and confused.

That is why I suggest that, if you are a beginner at meditation, you should first try to find that part of your life in which you are present already. Feel into the spirit of that place and build your meditation practice off that spot. If you do, it will teach you more about meditation than any book will do.

Practice

Pause for a moment to consider your daily life and ask yourself in which activity are you most fully present, without even trying to be, without even making a special effort to be here and now.

The answer could be anything: bowling, using the calculator, cooking, or rocking your child to sleep. What brings you to the present is as subjective as who you are.

Nevertheless, to be certain, give yourself the following test:

- Is it something you do for its own sake? Or do you obsess about the result?
- Do you feel relaxed and settled afterward, or are you more stressed out?
- Is your relationship to that activity direct and simple, or is it a complicated thing?

Take a few minutes to run through various activities in your mind until you come to one that fits. Don't get the idea beforehand that you know exactly what it is, or what it *ought* to be. You may surprise yourself. Being present is entirely natural, and therefore lacking in self-consciousness, so don't assume that you already know what your personal present moment is.

I took this test myself this morning, after not having thought of it in several years. I was surprised to find that my present moment came each morning after my shower when I turned on my computer and waited for it to boot up. During those forty-five seconds or so, I just look out the window at the yard, noting the weather, whether the snow has melted, and whether there are any animals near the pond. This morning the marsh hawk was back, sitting in the sapling by the bridge. Which is almost a haiku.

This Is It

I once saw a cartoon depicting two Buddhist monks seated side by side in a meditation hall. An older monk was muttering something to a younger monk out of the corner of his mouth. The young monk looked dumbfounded. The caption read: "Nothing happens next. This is it."

One of the most difficult challenges in meditation is to let go of expectation and experience the present for what it is. Ironically, this may take some effort to master. In a Zen Buddhist monastery the traditional wisdom says that it's not likely to happen before the middle day of a seven-day silent retreat. During the first three days, there is usually a lot of artificial effort. One tries very hard to focus the mind, and when it wanders, one feels obliged to drag it kicking and screaming back. After all, during a meditation retreat, that's the name of the game. If you're not meditating, then there's no excuse for just sitting around all day.

Eventually, the mind stops craving excitement. But first it has to pass through boredom, like traveling across the desert to an oasis on the other side. At first you weren't bored with meditation because you were expecting something. You were impatiently waiting for something to happen. Then, when it became apparent that nothing was going to happen—just more of the same: breath, numbers, stray thoughts—you began to think, "So what! What's the big deal? I must be missing something."

But you are not missing anything, and that's the whole point. It's so simple, so plain, that, in the beginning, it's actually quite difficult to practice it. The present is just what it is.

How Long, How Much?

When you are alone you can meditate as long as you like. In a group you have to agree beforehand. I have found that fifteen or twenty minutes is about right for most people, but you could also meditate for four breaths, which takes most people less than a minute to perform. You could even start a group that meets regularly for one four-breath meditation. Probably you would want such a group to consist of people who live together or who meet regularly for some other purpose, at work, for instance, because otherwise it would seem like too much trouble to come together for so short a period of time. The point is this: do not become fixated on length as a measure of how well you are meditating or how much benefit you are going to get from it.

Once, years ago, I found myself in the grips of a misunderstanding on this matter. Somehow I developed the idea that only if I meditated constantly would I derive any real benefit from it. My friends and family thought I was nuts. I was irritable when my meditation was disturbed, resentful of the many other demands on my attention. Eventually, I divorced my wife and became a Buddhist monk and the director of a Zen center in New York City where meditation was my job. As a monk I was still expected to attend all the retreats at the monastery where I had trained, and, in addition, I had retreats of my own to conduct. I doubt if anyone in New York was meditating more than I was during that period, but still nothing happened.

One day a friend of mine asked me point-blank what it was I was trying to achieve. "I'm trying to be in the present. I'm trying to wake up and live my life," I answered. "Then you're doing a lousy job," my friend replied. "All you do is meditate. What kind of life is that?" And, of course, he was right.

After that, I started leaving the center for an hour at midday and going to Central Park to lie in the sun. On Saturday night I rode the subway down to Greenwich Village, had a beer at a restaurant bar, and listened to the pleasant din of voices or struck up a conversation of my own. I bought a pair of Rollerblades and started skating by the river. And, much to my surprise, quite on their own, there came moments when I felt completely present, without any effort at all, other than perhaps the decision just to let myself be.

Discipline

When you meditate you should focus on nothing but counting the breath from one to four. Very simple, though it
requires some effort. However, you will get yourself tied up
in knots if you think you can accomplish this by an act of
will. It's more like learning to ride a bicycle.

When you are learning to ride a bike, you fall off a lot.
You learn to ride by getting right back on. It takes time, but
after a while you learn the kind of relaxed balance mixed
with forward momentum that constitutes riding a bicycle,
and you can perform the action without any self-conscious
effort or concentration. You don't need to say to yourself,
"Now I will lean my body slightly to the right. Now left."
You do it naturally.

It may take some effort to get to this point with your
meditation, so you need to be gentle with yourself. Imagine
how difficult it would be if, in learning to ride a bicycle, you
burdened yourself with the idea of discipline. It would be as

if your father stood off to one side and cried, "You're lazy!" every time you fell.

When I suggest that you focus on nothing but counting the breath from one to four, I simply mean that you ought not to waste your time and energy on thoughts like, "I don't have the discipline for this." Just return to one when you find your mind wandering. That's discipline enough.

Master What Is Simple

Some people may be offended by the simplicity of this practice. They may feel it is too easy or watered-down. But how many people can actually practice what is simple? There is an ancient Chinese story which illustrates this point.

Once there was a man of letters, a poet, who made the journey to visit a meditation master to see what wise thing he might have to say. Arriving at the mountain where the master lived, he discovered him meditating in a tree.

"It looks dangerous up there," said the man.

"It looks far more dangerous where you are," said the master.

With this, the poet thought, This man must be enlightened. So he asked the master, "What is the essence of the Way?"

"Avoid evil. Practice good. And purify your heart each day," answered the master.

"But every three-year old child knows that little rhyme," said the poet.

"Maybe so," said the master. "But even a man of eighty cannot do it."

Again and again I encounter people—many of them teachers of one meditative technique or another—who have this reaction. Often they have mastered complex rituals, arcane practices, postures, or visualizations that have been passed down from one teacher to another in the traditions of the East, and that they feel are necessary in order to practice meditation. Sometimes they have practiced complex "preliminary" practices just to get to meditation. Yet they have not mastered the simplest thing of all: letting go of everything they know to experience the present here and now. It has been so long since they had a profound, simple view of their "beginner's mind," they no longer even remember that it is there.

Not to worry, however. The beginner's mind is never lost. And you needn't worry yourself over all the various teachings of the meditative traditions of East and West. It is enough to practice what is simple. Even if you later go on to master what is seemingly more complicated, more impressive, or difficult to do, if you forget the simplicity of merely being present, without ritual, without thinking, without ideas, it won't matter that you have mastered them. You will have forgotten the one essential thing.

Reed Grass

There are some reed grasses along the edge of the little pond that skirts our property in Woodstock. When it snows, the flakes collect on the dry blades, making them bend toward the ground. But always there comes a point when each grass blade has collected as many snowflakes as it can bear, and at that moment the blade dips suddenly and they all slide off. I have watched this happen many times.

At least once a day, each of us experiences something analogous to this. It happens in the moment when we fall asleep. The mind relaxes, the body goes slack, and all the little worries of the day slide off. For most of us, this happens naturally, without any effort at all.

The problem is that few of us are able to do this while we are awake. Nowhere is this more apparent than when we meditate. Many times when we sit down to count the breath, that very act seems to call forth a veritable blizzard of anxieties and physical tics. Sometimes we feel over-whelmed by what may seem like an avalanche of all the stored up tensions and worries of the day. This often gives rise to the impression, on the part of beginners, that medi-tation makes them worse, not better. But this is an illusion.

We normally keep ourselves distracted by other things. Once we sit down to meditate, the distractions cease and we are unprotected. Nothing has changed. We are simply more acutely aware of our underlying state of mind. A similar thing happens to people who suffer from insomnia. Once you are lying in bed in a darkened room, if you can't sleep, you are far more likely to be plagued by doubt or fear.

To learn how to let go of tensions and worries during meditation takes practice, but you can begin right away, by realizing first of all that fighting only makes it worse. The person who suffers from insomnia understands this lesson. Struggling against wakefulness only makes you more awake. In the same way, in meditation, fighting tension and anxiety only makes matters worse.

A therapist once told me the story of a man who came to him saying, "I'm worried about how much anxiety I have. I'm afraid I'll have a heart attack."

"Is your heart healthy?" asked the therapist.

"Yes," said the man. "That's not the problem. It's the anxiety that's got me so upset."

We are all a little bit like this. By meditating we learn to give ourselves a break. We learn not to amplify the prob-lems we have or invent ones we don't. The secret lies in yielding like a grass blade, and being patient like a grass blade, too. No problem. Just release yourself from worries one after another by returning to the breath. If you continue doing this, there will come a moment when, quite naturally, even gracefully, they all slide off.

Looking at a Star

The present is something you follow, not something you possess or own. If you become too fixated on the breath, on counting the numbers from one through four, you will find that they become suddenly that much more difficult to follow. Instead, try looking at them as you would a star.

If you look directly at a star, you will find that you cannot see it as clearly as when you look just to one side of it. In the same way, if you do not become overly invested in counting each number with perfect clarity, if you downscale your expectations just slightly, you will find that each number becomes that much more clear.

Meditation is a kind of paradox. The harder you try to grasp it, the further away it goes. The reason is simple. Meditation is the natural condition of our minds. Observing that condition changes it because it introduces an element of self-consciousness it otherwise wouldn't have. That element of self-consciousness removes us from whatever activity we are presently engaged in. Washing the dishes, we think to ourselves, "I am washing dishes," and suddenly we replace all the immediate tactile sensations of actually washing dishes with the "virtual" image of ourselves washing them. It's as if we are standing off to one side watching someone else do them. Only that someone else is ourselves. Naturally, it's pretty hard to get much real satisfaction from doing things this way. (Imagine if we tried to have sex like that.)

The situation is basically a comical one. Because we doubt the inherent worth of our immediate experience, we miss the boat. We miss the boat we are already riding in.

No Path

Despite what might be gathered from reading any number of meditation manuals, meditation does not involve a path. Not a *real* path in any case.

When we start meditating we usually don't have the feeling of experiencing much success. If we are to keep going, it becomes necessary for us to invent some story line about the future, wherein, at some point we will "get it." It becomes necessary to invent a path. At various stages along that path, we tell ourselves, there will be guides and markers, until finally, when we reach the end, we will understand what meditation is all about. This is what keeps us going. If we are studying with a teacher, that teacher may even help us along with our fantasy by saying such things as "It takes a long time to master Zen," or "You can become a senior student when you've practiced for seven years."

Some meditators, including many teachers, think of this as a necessary deception, but I do not believe that this is so. That it may be inevitable, however, I will freely admit. It is inevitable for us to imagine ourselves making progress at meditation. If we are to continue doing it from one year to the next, most of us will need some sense that we are getting the hang of it, that we have undergone some important change since we started, that our lives are better, more focused, that we are more resistant to stress or anger. But is this the point? I think not.

Over and over again to come back to the present moment—*this* is the point of meditation. It is always the same point, though it appears to happen at different places and times. Were we to call it a path, we would violate its nature. Were we to call it a journey, we would only be imposing our own set of illusions on what is really there. The truth of our experience is nonlinear. The present is always here and now. You don't progress to it, or graduate from it.

Meditation doesn't make us better or worse or different than we are, it only wakes us up. Certainly it is human to imagine such a journey, just as it is human to take pleasure in seeing the shapes of gods and goddesses in the stars. But to be liberated, to be fully present here and now, finally we must understand that there is only one star ... and another star ... and another. Beautiful, beautiful stars.

Part 2

Getting Settled

The Red-Tailed Hawk

Something has disturbed the backyard stillness, sending a skein of dry, powdery snowflakes down from a branch halfway up the maple. Because of this, we catch the very moment a red-tailed hawk opens his wings to clutch the air.

At first he looks heavy, the wingbeats labored. But after a moment or so he rises above the trees and ceases to flap his wings. From there on, his flight appears effortless. It is hard to imagine that he has anything to do with the ground.

In the sky above the yard, he seems to make no effort beyond the slight tilt of his body into the wind, but even that seems more designed for the joy of flying than for any other purpose. To look at the way he floats, you would think that all of nature in her great circle were perpetually idle, with nothing left to do.

In our day to day lives seldom do we ever experience a moment when we can just let go of everything. Almost always there is some sense of obligation or responsibility. There are people to see and mouths to feed and miles to go before we sleep. And that is why we so seldom experience the present moment in all its radical simplicity, free and clear. Freedom, if we remember it at all, is a feeling we had in childhood. Our lives are levied on every side.

What would happen if we could have, just for a second, the experience of freedom here and now? What would happen if we could exist with complete simplicity, as a child does, as all of nature does, outside of time? Would the world change? Would everything be different? Wouldn't it actually be like looking at the same world, but from the standpoint of freedom instead of being bound?

Meditation doesn't take us on a journey to some other dimension or to a faraway land. It only shows us who and what and where we really are. The feeling we get when we meditate, of having made a leap or a journey, is only a measure of how far we have strayed from ourselves in the first place in the busyness and distraction of our day to day lives. The journey of meditation, then, is not a forward movement but a traveling back, to where we really are, to where we really exist. It's a nonjourney, a leap that isn't there.

Concentration

When we meditate, we look at one thing, and that one thing is the breath as it comes and goes from the body. Counting the breaths from one to four offers us a kind of feedback for that experience—a way of keeping track of it, of measuring the fluctuations in our concentration from one moment to the next. If we are able to follow the breath without losing count, then that tells us that we are concentrating well. If the counting is constantly interrupted by other thoughts, that tells us that our concentration is poor.

What most of us perceive as the crucial factor in meditation, then, is concentration. On a day when we are concentrating well, we will experience meditation as successful. On the other hand, when our concentration is poor, we may wonder why we bothered to meditate at all. Learning to meditate, it would seem, has everything to do with concentration. Or does it? What is concentration, really?

First of all, concentration must have an object. Concentration is the act of collecting the awareness in one place and turning the focus of that collected awareness on a single thing. To concentrate, then, means to look at one thing, to think one thought. Really, concentration is a measure of density.

One day, standing at the corner of 88th and Amsterdam in Manhattan, it occurred to me that living in the buildings immediately around me were as many people as lived in my hometown. In the same way, the mind that is fully concentrated is a very dense mind, a mind in which all the thoughts are collected in one place.

Because the initial method we use to meditate involves concentrating on the breath, it is easy to get the impression that concentration is what meditation is all about. But that is hardly so. Concentration is an act of will. Meditation, ultimately, is not.

Counting the breath from one to four gives us the useful illusion that there is something solid to take hold of in meditation. It provides us with a kind of mental handle for picking up the breath. The breath itself, however, is far more subtle and difficult to grasp. For there is nothing like a progression, a sequence, or a timeline when we are only meditating on the breath. Just one breath, and another breath, and another—on and on like that.

In breath counting, the numbers are an illusion. We invent them with the mind and assign them to the breaths in much the same way that we assign names to objects in the external world. For example, the word *cat*. Each language calls a cat by a different name. But the cat itself is something other than that name. Evoking the name won't produce a cat; and likewise, if you suddenly see a cat and for some reason can't remember what it is called, the animal won't disappear. *Cat* is just the name used for the sake of convenience.

In a similar vein, as long as we are counting the breaths, we aren't really touching them, but only the names (the numbers) by which they are called. To *touch* the breath, it becomes necessary to *follow* the breath instead. Fortunately, this tends to happen on its own.

After you have been counting the breath for a while, your concentration will begin to feel less artificial. Instead of having to strain to focus on counting from one to four, you will begin to relax into the rhythm of it. At that point, you may find that the counting is almost effortless to do.

Some people describe this as an enhanced feeling of slowness or of space. Because the frantic, grasping quality has now disappeared from your concentration, it is possible just to wait for each breath to come up before you count it—instead of feeling like *you* have to go to *it*.

Some mediators describe this as the feeling of waiting for something, but waiting with complete patience, without any anticipation or hurry at all. Really, when this happens, you are already *following* the breath. Soon, you may even begin to feel like a healthy person walking with a cane. Far from being a necessary support, it is more likely to trip you up instead. When that happens, you should toss the cane aside. After that, there is no effort at concentration but only following instead. Where the breath goes, you go. That is all.

Practice

If, after counting the breath for a while, your mind and body begin to feel clear and spacious and calm, then set the numbers aside and practice following instead.

Now close this book and try following the breath for a few minutes, just going wherever it goes.

Begin now.

How easy was it to sustain your connection to the breath without using the numbers as a prop? How long could you meditate just by following the breath in and out, without trying to force it or control it in any way?

As you may have discerned by now, the most valuable lesson in meditation is starting over. In the beginning, when you first started to count the breath, it was probably necessary to come back to one over and over again before you ever got to four. But by learning to let go and come back to the present each time your mind wandered, eventually you found that you could do it. You learned to meditate that way.

In learning to follow the breath we use the same method, returning to breath counting whenever we become distracted and lose that patient, spacious feeling that allows us just to follow the breath wherever it goes. Thus, a typical meditation session involves counting for a few minutes, then following the breath for the remainder of the time, returning to counting for a minute or two when necessary to recover that quiet, spacious mind.

Compared to counting, following is a less ego-driven, less goal-oriented form of meditation. In following the breath, there is still some *object* of meditation, but that object isn't something we try to grasp. It isn't even something we try to concentrate on. With a clear, composed mind, we simply follow where it goes. Think of it as a form of surrender. Surrender to the breath.

Shallow, Not Deep

Even experienced meditators sometimes fall into the trap of thinking that they must meditate "deeply" in order to benefit from the practice. Actually, just the opposite is true. If we meditate too deeply, we will most likely miss the point of meditation, which is simply to be aware of the present place and time. Thinking we must meditate deeply is like supposing that we can go deeper into a reflection of the moon by reaching below the surface of the water. The truth is, there is no reflection below the water. In just the same way, there is nothing below the surface of the mind. The surface is the mind.

Our minds are always "piercing" reality in the effort to grasp or "get" something. We are seldom able to accept things just the way they are. For this very reason, it is often extremely difficult to count the breaths from one to four, touching just briefly on each number without losing count and without reflecting self-consciously on what we are doing.

It is, likewise, rather difficult just to follow the breath with a light, clear, vivid awareness, unhurried by any thought of the next moment, or held back by clinging to the one that went before. Nevertheless, with practice it is possible to meditate this way.

Perhaps you have had the experience of waking well-rested on a Saturday morning. Your mind is alert, but you have not yet begun to think about the day. The sun is shining in the yard, and all around you is perfectly clear morning light. That alertness sustains itself without even trying. You may not even notice it except for the feeling of being rested and ready for the day.

The experience of meditation is something like that. When you meditate you are not trying to have any particular experience. You are simply awake. After having counted your breath from one to four for several minutes, quite without having aimed at that experience, you start to feel a kind of clarity and space surrounding each number as you count. It feels a little like having enough space to think, enough room to move and breathe, or simply "be."

Once we have begun meditating in this way it may take us a while to realize that we don't have to meditate deeply, that we can simply accept things as they are. There is nothing to get or reach for. The "depth" of meditation is right before our eyes.

Water Strider

If you take a walk along a stream during the summertime, in places where the stream is calm, you will probably see water striders, called "Jesus bugs" by some people because they appear to "walk on water."

These long-legged insects are able to move freely across the water, buoyed-up by its surface tension. They skate easily this way and that, upstream or down, each of their six legs making the slightest dimple on the surface of the stream. As a child I remember sitting by the drainage ditch in back of our house, watching these little fellows race back and forth across the surface reflections of summer clouds.

Like water, the present moment has its own surface tension, a kind of natural buoyancy or lightness of spirit that emerges when we stay with the moment, and don't allow ourselves to get sucked in by the various thoughts and impressions flowing through the mind. When we are able to maintain that kind of spirit, then the mind moves very lightly and easily with the breath.

Think of the water strider. Does it matter whether he skates over a cloud or over the open sky? To the water strider it is just the same. Likewise, if you maintain a light, easy attitude about what you are doing—if you don't make it too serious—you won't get consumed by thoughts and worries. You just skate across the surface, cloudy or fair.

Thoughts

What do you do about distracting thoughts that come up in meditation? The answer is, what do you normally do?

In our day to day lives stray thoughts are not the exception but the rule. Were you to take a brief inventory of the thoughts that pass through your mind during any given minute of time, you would doubtless be amazed at how disconnected and varied they are. Looking for the house keys, you briefly wonder why you cannot get more things done. Better wear black socks today. I wish I had more money. Shirley is a problem. I wonder what my ex-wife's new house looks like in Tennessee.

And yet, in spite of all this, we manage to get things done. We drive to work, wash dishes, hold meetings, or teach a classroom full of kids. We work water into clay and throw a pot. And we accomplish all of these things in exactly the same way, by repeatedly reorienting ourselves to the present moment, by coming back to the task at hand, back

to where we are. In fact, what we experience as the conti-
nuity of any activity—for instance, driving a car—is nothing more than the linkage of all the many hundreds,
perhaps thousands, of moments when our attention returns
to touch just briefly upon our immediate experience: the
varying pressure of the foot on the accelerator, the texture
of the road vibrating through the seat or the steering wheel,
slight variations in the distance between us and the car up
ahead.

Meditation is an activity performed solely for itself.
There are no built-in distractions. In driving a car, you
might feel distracted now and then by thoughts of where
you want to go, what you are going to do when you get
there, and whether you are late and might need to drive a
little faster. In meditation you aren't going anywhere at all.
There is no progress, nothing to look forward to, nothing to
dread. Only what is here and now. In this case, counting
and then following the breath. So the answer to the question of what to do with thoughts is simple: When your mind
wanders, bring it back to the breath. It's as difficult and as
simple as that.

Realistically, there may be times when nothing works,
when, for one reason or another, the rush of thoughts is
too powerful when you first sit down to meditate. Once,
shortly after we moved to Woodstock, my wife, Perdita,
told me that she was having trouble meditating at night.
At that time our children were ages three and two months.
Between caring for the two of them, she had her hands
full (quite literally) all day long, so when we had put the

children to bed and sat down to meditate, all the interrupted, unfinished thoughts poured back into her mind
like a torrent. The children were on different nap schedules, so our sitting time was the first moment she had for
reflection all day long, and she was starved for it.

She knew how much it helped just to sit calmly and
meditate, how much more renewed she felt afterward, but
she couldn't count to four even once without thinking of a
thousand different things. This frustration is a fairly common problem, both for parents of young children and for
people with demanding lifestyles or jobs. But the solution
is fairly simple.

The image of a torrent, a flooding stream, is instruc-
tive. Like a tornado or a hurricane, a flood is a force of
nature. If you live on a coastline or a river, you know that
there are certain things you can do to protect yourself from
rising water. But you also know that, if the force of that
water is powerful enough, there is nothing you can do. The
only solution is to ride it through. Eventually the water will
recede. And when the floodwater has all rushed by, the
stream will slow and become clear again.

Similarly, when you experience a flood of thoughts,
you're much better off just sitting there calmly while that
happens. You are only likely to hurt yourself if you try to
block them instead.

Boomerangs

The way to get rid of a boomerang is not to throw it but to leave it where it is and step over it. In the same manner, the way to get rid of troublesome thoughts, ones that keep coming back over and over again no matter how many times you throw them away, is not by using force.

As you meditate, more and more you will learn to distinguish between those anxieties, worries, or fears which are chronic, and those that can easily be set aside. One way to tell the difference is by noticing which ones come up over and over again.

In its natural state the mind is very fluid; the thoughts passing through it arise effortlessly and just as effortlessly subside. When one thought dominates, that means that it needs to be addressed. But how we address that thought in meditation is different from how we address it in psychotherapy or in our day to day lives. In psychotherapy, we look for the causes of such a thought. Why, we might ask ourselves, do I always feel depressed for days after having lunch with my brother? After talking with a therapist about these feelings for a few weeks or months, they will generally become clearer. On the other hand, our usual way of dealing with disturbing thoughts in our daily lives is just to suffer, to endure them for as long as they last, or perhaps to try to push them from our minds, which usually only makes them worse. In meditation we don't do any of these things.

In meditation we leave a boomerang right where it is. Lying on the ground like that, somebody is less likely to get hurt than if we start tossing it recklessly about in the attempt to get rid of it. In meditation, when we see a boomerang, we just say, "There's a boomerang," and leave it where we found it.

As simple as this is, the effect of doing this is remarkable. By recognizing the thought for what it is, we give it the respect it demands. But because we do this without giving it more energy than it already has, it becomes less troublesome. In meditation we don't add to the burden of a problem by thinking we have to solve it or get rid of it here and now. We have another option. For the time being we can choose to leave it where it is. In other words, we can do nothing at all.

In doing so, we soon discover that once troublesome thoughts no longer have fear or anxiety latched onto them, they become easier to bear. We might even find a better solution to them later on.

Staying Dry

While it is important not to get sucked into the myriad thoughts and feelings that flow through the mind at any given moment, it is also important not to let yourself just fly off into fantasy.

Returning to the image of a water strider, we may observe that its nature to stay on the surface of the water, not to fly off into the sky. In the same way, it is important to stay grounded when you meditate.

The problem comes when we settle into a habitual thought pattern, turning *grounded*ness into *rooted*ness. When that happens, you will quickly find that you have forgotten to count or follow your breaths. Before you know it, you have become stuck in some familiar pattern of thought.

How then do we skate lightly across the surface of the present without flying off into fantasy, but also without getting stuck in feelings of unhappiness or fear? How do we maintain a balance between heavy and light? Once again, look at nature.

A water strider's legs stick to the water without getting *stuck* to it. How does he do that? If you look carefully, you will find that, despite the fact that it lives on water, the water strider manages to keep himself quite dry. It is this dryness that keeps him fastened to the water. Doubtless, if he became thoroughly wet, he would get stuck, struggling to free himself like a spider in a stream.

How does all of this translate into meditation? Think of the word *dryness*. In addition to meaning "free of moisture, not wet," *dry* means "lacking embellishment; plain; matter-of-fact." These words, which sound quite boring at first, actually point to the secret of meditation. For if we maintain a spirit of plainness in counting our breaths from one to four, we will soon notice that it is easier to maintain our focus from one number to the next. It is easier to keep ourselves buoyed-up by the present. Likewise, if we don't embellish the present with fantasies like, "My life is going better since I've started to meditate," it is easier to stay focused on following the breath.

When you think of it, being with the present is actually rather matter-of-fact. No need to make a big production of it. Just be there. Not too heavy, not too light.

Trusting Your Problems

Meditation is sometimes thought to be a form of escapism, a way of opting out of the practical, hard-edge aspects of life. But I always laugh when I hear criticisms of this kind. It seems to me that the people who think that they can escape their problems through meditation have a far more inflated notion of it than I do. Anyone who has spent any time at all on the cushion knows for a fact that, even though you may temporarily set your problems aside while you meditate, they come right back the moment you unfold your legs.

Meditation doesn't change who we are. It doesn't change our basic situation, or where we work and live. And while it may often make our problems seem smaller or more manageable, it certainly doesn't make them go away. If that were the case, everyone would meditate, no questions asked.

Part of learning to meditate involves learning to trust your problems. Often, when people first start meditating, they get the idea that if they don't constantly monitor their problems, those same problems will momentarily subside, only to spring back up again, a month or a day later, in some infinitely more worrisome form than before. It takes a while to learn that, if something really *is* a problem, meditation isn't going to make it go away. The problem will reassert itself as something that needs to be dealt with at the appropriate moment later in time. If it doesn't resurface, then there was never anything to worry about. If meditating for twenty minutes or so makes your problem go away, then it wasn't much of a problem to begin with. You've done yourself a favor by just letting it go.

This is one of the principal benefits of meditation from a psychological point of view. It helps us to distinguish what really is a problem from what might just be caused by obsessive preoccupation or by stress.

Though meditation is a wakeful state, as I have mentioned before, its effect is sometimes just like falling asleep. When you lie down to rest at night, your body relaxes and your mind lets go of the tension it has accumulated during the day. If this were not so—if you had no way of emptying the mind and body of its accumulated sorrow—then life would be impossible to live. As it is, we are all, to varying degrees, gifted with this small miracle of erasure that comes nightly to refresh our souls. And yet, that nightly reprieve does nothing to mitigate the effects of problems that might need urgent attention. If they are real, chances are we will wake up thinking about them.

In the same way, briefly forgetting everything else just to follow the breath isn't going to hinder your ability to cope with problems that need to be addressed. It's all right to relax and enjoy the momentary break, just as you enjoy a nap or a good night's sleep.

Once you have learned to trust in the solidity of your problems—once you've learned that real problems don't just go away—then you can learn to relax and let go more fully when you meditate. Once you've learned that, the present moment may very well begin to feel like an island vacation away from it all. The time you meditate will begin to feel as though you are relaxing in the warmth and energy of the sun.

Coffee Beans

When I was in college I developed the habit of staying up late at night either walking or reading, so that in the mornings I was frequently quite tired and had to drink lots of strong black coffee. On one such morning I arrived at Deh Chun's house for a visit. When he offered me some weak black tea warmed up over his woodstove, I politely declined. He looked at me questioningly, so I explained that I was used to drinking coffee.

Though Deh Chun grew almost all of his own food and was fairly fanatical on the subject of what constituted a proper diet, he never criticized the way I lived. Friendship, it seemed, was the most important thing. So the next time I arrived for a morning visit, he announced that he had prepared some coffee for me.

I was so relieved. Things often went very slowly in the little house in Monteagle. In the winter it was quite cold in the room where we sat next to the stove, so the promise of

a good cup of coffee was doubly welcome. But when he lifted the lid on the pot (he had no kettle), I was surprised to
see only water. "Instant," I thought. "Oh, well." Then he
started to pour the water into one of the small bowls he
used as teacups. At that point I peered more closely into
the water and realized there was coffee after all. Four
beans, to be precise. He had boiled them for almost half an
hour in preparation for my visit.

I wanted to laugh, but Deh Chun looked quite serious,
so all I said was that I had never seen coffee prepared that
way before. "Best way!" he said, without even a grin, and
offered me the bowl. It was like drinking ... well, hot water,
in which the faint hint of real coffee lingered, on the verge
of disappearing altogether like a morning dream.

The strange thing is, years later in my mind's eye, I can
still see with perfect clarity those four coffee beans floating
in water. Sometimes the memory comes back to me when I
am feeling very stressed out over something, or when I have
trouble calming myself down at the beginning of a period
of meditation. I still drink coffee, three, sometimes four
cups a day, but when I think of Deh Chun's "coffee," I have
to laugh at how complicated I sometimes make my life. And
at how often I forget to be simple. That laughter is a kind
of medicine, and almost a meditation in itself.

Stop Tying Knots

A certain yoga teacher once told me that the perfectly enlightened mind was one in which all the knots and kinks and coils had come undone. "How do you do that?" I asked her. I expected her to explain some sort of postural technique. But she only laughed and said, "Stop tying knots."

The lesson of the present moment is to stop doing violence to ourselves. Almost all of us have some dearly held notion of how things "ought to be." On the one hand, such ideas lead to progress. Every day we strive to make things better and better. However, the down side of this approach is that it makes us habitually dissatisfied with the present. Happiness, love, a good home life, always lie just beyond our grasp. So, even as it seems that we are motivating ourselves to improve the world, we are actually tying knots.

How do we get ourselves to stop doing this? The main thing is to realize that it requires *less* effort, not more. It requires us to recognize all the many ways in which we make simple things difficult.

For instance, after reading this book you may decide that it is the answer to all of your problems. "It's just like he said," you tell your friends. "We just have to be fully present in our lives." And so, beginning tomorrow morning, and on every other morning thereafter, you get up at six A.M. to read a chapter of this book and then meditate for thirty minutes or so. But then, inevitably, your enthusiasm wanes. One night you stay out late, and the next morning you don't get up to meditate. "I shouldn't have stayed up so late," you tell yourself. "I should have gotten up to meditate. Now my mind is a complete muddle, and I wouldn't know the present if it bit me on the ass."

You'd do better not to meditate at all.

The secret of not tying knots is the same in meditation as in most things in life. When you meditate, just meditate. When you don't, just don't. Once you understand this, you can meditate in a way that will loosen, not tighten all your knots.

Seriousness

When I first went to live in the monastery where I trained, I was filled with the grandeur and the seriousness of following a spiritual path. I had left my wife to become a monk, and several people, including the abbot, had remarked to me how impressed they were with the sacrifices I had made. But when, after two weeks, my seriousness showed no signs of letting up, the monks conspired to teach me a lesson.

In those days the monastery schedule had not yet become fully Americanized, and so it was especially rigid. Once every two weeks there was a rest day. The remainder of the time we meditated and worked. That year we were seriously understaffed, so everyone had to work overtime. It was still winter, but there had been a few warm days already and the sap was ready to flow, so all the trees had to be tapped in preparation for the maple syrup season. The mountainside was steep and the snow was still three feet deep in places, so the going was slow and hard. By the time the first rest day arrived, everyone was exhausted. Most people slept in, a few missed breakfast altogether, and by nightfall everyone still looked exhausted.

Perhaps because of this, the abbot decided to throw a little party. A wealthy Japanese patron had donated a case of sake to the monastery that day, and so, in keeping with a long tradition of Japanese Zen monasticism, the abbot decided to temporarily lift the prohibition against alcohol. If you are of the school that says that alcohol has its proper uses, you would have seen that this was clearly one of them. Everyone's mood lifted within moments of the first glass, and within an hour people were laughing again and making jokes about the work.

There was a problem, however, because we had to be up again at 4:30 the next morning. Just because we had received the donation of sake didn't mean we could just throw the whole monastery schedule out the window. "You're the *jokei*," the abbot told me. "You'd better get to bed. Otherwise, you might sleep through your alarm clock and have to kneel all morning at the entrance to the meditation hall, wearing white *tabi* socks as a sign of contrition."

This part intrigued me. There's no greater fanatic for ritual than a convert, so at the mention of this seemingly arcane rule, I had to know more. "Sometimes the *jokei* [the monk whose job it is to wake the others up] oversleeps," he explained. "This is a serious infraction of the monastery rules, even though it sometimes gives the monks a little extra sleep. When this happens, that monk is expected to address the other monks in a loud voice, proclaiming his offense. Thereafter, he is to dress in formal robes and kneel all morning at the entrance to the meditation hall."

After this explanation the abbot smiled at me broadly and rose to go back to his quarters. I also rose and announced my intention to depart. I had to be up early, I explained. Otherwise the rest of them would oversleep.

The monks were incensed. Two of them grabbed me by the shoulders and pulled me forcibly back to the low table where we had all been sitting on the floor. "Just where do you think you're going?" the head monk demanded. "You don't understand anything at all."

"Yeah," said another. "Didn't you see what he was saying? We don't have to get up till seven."

I wasn't convinced. The monks were always hazing me because I didn't know anything about the monastery rules. This could be just another one of their tricks, I thought. They're just trying to get me in trouble with the abbot. So I pulled myself away and went back to my room.

As it turned out, I barely slept at all. First of all, my alarm clock was missing. Someone had raced along the outdoor verandah from the meal hall to my room and taken it before I arrived. Now *I* was incensed. It became a matter of pride.

Predictably, nobody would lend me an alarm clock, so I had to go searching in the monastery store room, where I remembered seeing one that somebody had left after a lay retreat. But with that problem solved, I found that I was too agitated to sleep. It turned out, that was a good thing.

Soon I could hear the heavily accented, slightly drunken voice of Essan, one of the Japanese monks in residence, outside my door. Looking through a crack in the doorway, I could see that he and another Japanese monk, Yossan, held a long piece of rope. Fearing that they intended to tie me up so I couldn't ring the wake-up bell, I barricaded myself inside the room using my reading table and bed. But that was not what they had in mind.

Instead, they tied my doorknob to the one across the hallway, so that I couldn't open the door more than half an inch. At first I thought of cutting the rope, but the blade of my Swiss army knife wasn't long enough. So for a long time I just sat on my bed and thought.

In the morning, when Essan woke up he found the door to his room tied shut. Had he not been laughing so hard, he might have realized that he could free himself by removing the hinges from the door.

Everyone was relieved that I had allowed them to sleep late. After all that had happened, it seemed like the only thing to do. At breakfast, I apologized in a loud voice to the monks, and everyone laughed. Afterward, I put on my white socks and was headed to the meditation hall, but the head monk stopped me. It wasn't necessary, he said. Apparently the abbot had noticed Essan's door tied shut and gotten quite a laugh out of that. As far as they were concerned, the lesson had been learned.

Do You Meditate Every Day?

Since I stopped being a monk, I have lost track of how many different people have asked me that question. It is easy to answer it truthfully: the answer is no. Usually, however, I am more interested in what made people ask. I have noticed that many people find it necessary to add a certain moralistic dimension to meditation—an attitude which has no real place in meditation and, if anything, only adds to their list of problems. When this happens, meditation, which is actually very simple, which happens from moment to moment quite naturally, becomes neurotic instead.

Most meditators, I have discovered, are secretly keeping score. "I meditated last night so this morning it's all right to feel good." The fact is, it's all right to feel good whether you have meditated or not. Likewise, there is absolutely nothing wrong with feeling lousy, or even depressed, on a day when you have meditated. It's even all right to feel lousy *while* you are meditating. It doesn't mean that you are meditating wrong.

Meditation is not about keeping score, nor is it about obsessively looking for a particular result. Meditation only means being in your life. On some days your life is organized in such a way that it is impossible to meditate. Perhaps you are sick, or you are caring for an infant and only want to sleep as soon as he or she does. Maybe you are on vacation and having too much fun. The point is this: to be more free of anxiety, more able to be happy in the present moment, it doesn't make sense to add to your problems, so don't let thoughts of "I ought to" or "I shouldn't have" invade meditation. Meditate when you can, when you most enjoy it or most need it, and don't get too fixated on keeping to a fixed schedule or achieving a particular result.

Not long ago, at a party in New York, I happened to run into a man I had not seen in many years. In his late fifties, he had been practicing Zen meditation for more than thirty years. At one time we had studied at the same monastery, but he had long since moved on. After we had caught up on old times, he asked, "So, do you still meditate?" And when I said yes, he asked, "Do you meditate every day?" Both could have been innocent inquiries, but I detected anxiety and depression behind them. His eyes narrowed and it was clear to me that part of him wished that he wasn't asking this question, and that he didn't feel the need to know the answer.

It made me sad to see how much his relationship to meditation was still defined by fear. He was still stuck in the same sad place, still driven to meditate as if he were trying to save his life—as if meditation were some kind of respiration device he was afraid to do without. And I realized that meditation was, and always had been, merely another thing he clung to, another thing he used to keep himself unhappy. Paradoxically, it had become another way to keep himself from living now.

Summoning the Present

After you have been meditating for some years, you can find yourself in the moment just by summoning the present. When you have reached that point, often you can enter meditation right away, without the exercise of any artificial method whatsoever, so your practice can occur anywhere, at any time.

Of course, by the expression "summoning the present," what we mean is actually a kind of joke. You can't summon what's already there. It would be like calling out to yourself, and then answering yourself, or like touching your own head to make sure that it was there. So you might also call summoning the present the art of laughing as well.

The longer we just sit still with the present, watching the breath flow in and out of the body, the more we realize that the present is always there—it is our *awareness* of it that comes and goes. It's as close and intimate as our own two hands. If you're not using them, you may not notice the hands. But they are there just the same—at your sides, in your pockets, or maybe clasped behind your back. If someone carrying a heavy package says, "Give me a hand," you can present them right away. Summoning the present works in much the same way. It is like telling yourself to give yourself a hand.

The laughter, of course, comes when we begin to realize how often we lose sight of the present, even though it is always there, right before our eyes. To resuscitate an old cliché, "it's as plain as the nose on your face." Only, like the nose, we look past it. Like the nose, it's almost too close to see.

How, then, do we summon the present? It works like this.

At a certain moment we realize that we have slipped, that our awareness has faltered and we have lost sight of it. That thought is immediately followed by another one—we must get the present back. Then the whole thing falls apart in laughter, like a joke whose punch line comes sooner than we thought, because we remember that we can't get back what we already have.

When that happens, we suddenly become short-circuited in the act of deceiving ourselves. We fail to sustain the illusion of a present moment that comes and goes. So we laugh.

What does this feel like? The best way I have found to describe it is a sense of folly mixed with mirth. It takes some years of meditating to be able to laugh at ourselves like that. It's not something you can fake. But when it's finally funny, you will know it. Once you realize how simple meditation is, you will know how often we forget to be simple, and what a funny thing that is.

The Spring

When you begin meditating you invite a certain kind of frustration into your life. Once you begin to cultivate some clarity of mind, for the first time you begin to notice when it is cloudy.

When that happens, you can still find clarity if you can touch your wakeful mind. This may sound obscure, but once you learn how to do it, it is as simple as reaching your finger down to touch the floor.

From the standpoint of the present moment, we are always aware of everything. Some basic clarity is always there, no matter what we say or think or do. It is like a mirror reflecting clouds. The clouds do not make the mirror less clear than if it reflected a face. Our minds are the same way.

Once many years ago my college girlfriend and I went hiking in the mountains. After walking a long way, we stopped for lunch beside a small spring-fed lake. We had brought food, but nothing to drink. When I complained about this and wanted to head back, she said it wasn't necessary. There was water all around.

I looked at the pond and found nothing very appetizing about the condition of the water. Moreover, as a child I had been indoctrinated against drinking pond water by countless camp counselors and scoutmasters. But Sally slipped out of her clothes and waded right into the lake. She would swim underwater for twenty or thirty seconds, coming up in a different place each time. Finally, she emerged from a place about ten yards from the far shore and shouted, "Here it is."

I wasn't sure what she meant, but I took off my own clothes and swam to where she was. She took my hand and we swam down a dozen or so feet until a wave of cool water struck my face. She had found the spring that fed the lake.

Years later I discovered that our minds are just the same. Quite often the surface looks green and murky, but at bottom there is something clear. Sally had found the spring by swimming in the direction of the coolest water. You can find clarity the same way when you meditate.

When you notice you are sleepy, simply stay with that thought. The part of your mind that notices you are sleepy is, by definition, the part that is the most awake. After a few moments of thinking how sleepy you are, you will find your mind is much more alert and clear. It feels much like sipping clear water off the bottom of a cloudy lake.

Don't Believe It

By this point it is probably unnecessary to state again that meditation happens now, not in the future or the past. Understanding that meditation doesn't happen in the future is easy for most people to grasp. The future is not yet real. But to understand that it shouldn't happen in the past is generally more difficult. How, you might ask, *could* it happen in the past? In my experience, there are two ways.

The first is by reliving old experiences when we meditate, especially those that involve meditation. When that happens, we become wrapped in a kind of nostalgic reverie that, because it concerns the *memory* of meditation, may give us the illusion of actually meditating now. Especially when we are having difficulty staying focused, it may be tempting to think of past occasions when we meditated well. The problem with this is that it sets the present against the past. I call this the Golden Age phenomenon.

Once you have meditated for a month or more, you

too will have a Golden Age of meditation: a particular time when the world was freshly made and meditation seemed to happen on its own. When we set meditative experiences against one another in this way, labeling one of them as satisfactory and the other not, we forget the whole purpose of meditation, which is to be present to whatever is happening now, regardless of the content of that experience. We forget that meditation is mind itself, not *state* of mind.

The second way of meditating in the past generally involves a lot of reading. It happens when you study a particular meditative tradition such as Buddhism or yoga or Christian contemplation and become attached to stories about great masters of the past. You repeat their words to yourself while you meditate, and relive episodes from their lives. I call this vicarious meditation, and, supposing you were sufficiently impressed with some of the stories herein, it could even happen with this book.

Once a friend of my mine, another student of Deh Chun, asked him about the Buddha's enlightenment. Deh Chun leaned over close to him and whispered, "Don't believe it." Did he mean that the Buddha's enlightenment wasn't real? I think not. But apparently he thought it had become a burden for my friend.

I like to think of Deh Chun's statement when I catch myself getting caught up in some story about the past. Whatever it is, don't believe it, I tell myself, whether it's true or not.

Housefly

One night I was meditating alone in the room where I do my writing. I don't recall the day being particularly special. I had been working on a book and things were fairly calm.

After I had been meditating for a while, I found that I had been staring for a long time at a housefly that had landed on the wall. I was no longer counting or following the breath. In fact, it didn't seem that I was doing much of anything at all. I was just looking at a fly.

The fly was completely still. It hadn't moved the whole time I was watching it. Strictly speaking, I wasn't even aware of watching it anymore. It was just that the fly was all there was to look at on the smooth white wall, so that was naturally where my attention fell.

Then, suddenly, it flew away. All at once it was gone and I was left looking at ... what? Not the wall. Not really. I had ceased to look at the wall while I was looking at the fly, and so when the fly left there was a kind of gap, a momentary lapse in something. Perhaps that something was myself. I don't know how long the moment lasted, but I assume it was very short. In any event, in that gap there was nothing there. And yet ... I kept looking at it.

Here, of course, language fails. If I say that there was nothing there and no one looking at it, and yet that no one was myself ... looking at nothing ... then it all sounds hopelessly obscure. Really, all that happened was that one moment I was looking at a fly on the wall of my studio, and the next moment it was gone. Nothing there.

When I describe an experience such as this, most people will probably say, "So what? No big deal." And perhaps they are right. But I would be remiss if I didn't also mention that my meditation was always different after that night. Thereafter, in the midst of various troubles, there was always something trouble-free—a kind of lingering awareness of the dreamlike quality of human life, and a peacefulness within that dream.

I only mention this here because it's important to know that you don't need to have any visions of glowing lights or radiant deities in order to have a breakthrough in meditation. A fly will do.

Forgetting

In the language we have used to talk about meditation, *forgetting* is the term we use to describe meditation in which there is no theme, no method, and no technique. It is based on the understanding that, whether we know it or not, we are present already, and so ultimately there is nothing to do.

At this stage of meditation we forget to obsess about money, sex, psychological problems, regrets, hopes, fears, and other people's faults. We even forget to obsess about the breath. But there is some danger that we will use forgetting as an excuse for being impatient or for relaxing into a state of torpor, or even as an excuse for indulging in all sorts of fantasies and story lines instead of counting or following the breath. For that reason, I abide by the following rule, as a kind of safeguard, in my own meditation practice: *Always begin by counting, and then by following the breath.*

If you feel bored or impatient with these exercises, it

is a sure indication that you are not yet ready to practice forgetting. Otherwise, you'll end up like a flightless bird that leaps once or twice and then pretends to soar about the sky. In reality you will have never left the ground. Likewise, if you feel sleepy or uninspired, then that is not the time to devote yourself to forgetting. Return to counting until you are awake enough to follow the breath, and continue with that until you are present enough to meditate without any props.

How do you *know* that there are no props? How do you know when you are meditating freely, without method, theme, or technique? The answer is, you don't. When you meditate by forgetting, there is no awareness of anyone meditating—with or without using any method, theme, or technique. This is not the same as unconsciousness, however. Rather, it is a supremely wakeful state.

In this condition the mind doesn't become distracted by any thoughts or emotions or sensations that arise. It is merely present. When all else is forgotten, that radical simplicity is what remains.

Practice

Return to the beginning. Remember that meditation is not a journey forward, but back.

Go back to the moment before you began following the breath. Go further back to the moment before you began to count. Go back to the moment when you sat down and straightened your spine in preparation to meditate.

And stop.

Remain on that spot, without doing anything. Whatever comes to mind, let it pass. Whatever tension remains in the body, let it go. And accomplish these things by simply remaining still.

You will discover that all around you is in motion. Breath moves. Mind moves. Wind moves. There is the ticking of somebody's watch. But like a mountain, the body remains still. That stillness is not something that comes or goes, but is a reflection of our natural state. When distraction is over, when busyness has passed us by, at bottom this is who and what and where we really are.

During your meditation, or at odd moments in daily life, you may have glimpses of this stillness, which, strictly speaking, has nothing to do with rest or motion because it comes from a source so much deeper than that. At such moments, do nothing. Do not even tell yourself that you are there. Nothing needs to be added to such moments to make them better or more perfect. They are complete the way they are.

Afterward, you may want to ask yourself a simple question. What did you have to *do* to have that experience? If the answer is anything but nothing, you may very well have missed the point.

My Teacher's Light

The essence of the present moment, then, is to recognize it here and now, without recourse to any method whatsoever. But this is so hard to do that, almost always, we need some method to function as a bridge. The problem is that methods tend to become a thing in themselves, complete with trustees, custodians, even investors. So we use a method (counting and then following the breath) that is so simple that it naturally collapses upon itself at a certain point, leaving us in a state of presence—here and now. This is the point—the *only* point. If you forget this, your meditation will quickly degenerate into a set of beliefs or opinions about what you are doing. If you remember it, there is nothing else to do. Even so, it is important not to get arrogant about it.

At first the knowledge of presence is something we have to tell ourselves we know. It has a stuck-on quality, something like a peel-off label we affix to the act of meditation.

The label keeps coming off, so we have to keep sticking it back on again, which makes us frustrated. Sometimes it makes us boastful (as if, by letting others know how well we meditate, we could make it really so).

Later, when we have settled down a bit, we have glimpses of real presence in spite of ourselves, in spite of the self-conscious way we ordinarily look at the world. At first these glimpses may seem like nothing, because we cannot hold on to them or because they are impossible to define. But after a while we accept this. We get used to the fact that we are simply here.

Eventually we know it. But that knowledge comes from within us like an inner light. Others may not notice it, but we know instinctively that it is there. We know even before we think about it. So we don't have to think about it all the time. We simply are. In recent years I have found myself less and less impressed with spiritual teachers whose inner light illuminates whole rooms full of people. A light that bright overwhelms the other lights around it. It may feel wonderful to bask for a moment in the warmth of a spiritual floodlight, just as it feels wonderful for a child to be wrapped in her mother's arms. But I doubt that anyone realizes her spiritual nature by that alone.

Deh Chun's light shown so faintly that for more than a decade after his death I didn't even know that it was there. Sometimes, when I return home to Woodstock late at night, I think of it. My mother gave me a key chain with a tiny flashlight that lets me find the lock to the door. Sometimes I think of him when I see its light.

Part 3

Getting Together

The Alcove

Not long after I became a monk, my Japanese Zen teacher sent me back to New York City to take over the temple there. Outwardly, I accepted the post with modesty. Inwardly, I took it as indication that I had somehow arrived. Finally, I would be a teacher, a Zen master. At the time, it seemed my life was right on track.

My teacher did everything possible to encourage me in this folly. He dropped all sorts of hints and finally even said openly that I would "inherit" the temple. He did everything, that is, except one thing. He specified that I was to be the door person on Thursday nights.

Each Thursday the Zendo held an open house. Anyone, regardless of prior experience, was welcome to attend, so the people who came were mostly beginners. A few returned for a second or third week before drifting off. One or two each month became members. Some people were content to come each Thursday for years, paying the usual donation at the door, without ever attending any other Zendo functions.

I was already familiar with the job of door person. It was the very first job anyone was assigned when they voiced an interest in getting more involved in the practice. It was like being an intern, a bat boy, or an office clerk. While you might very well go on to become a meditation instructor, a monk, or possibly even a Zen master, this was where you started.

At first I thought it was a punishment, a penalty for having mismanaged a particularly crucial aspect of monastery protocol the month before. But my teacher seemed in such good spirits about the whole arrangement that I decided this interpretation didn't fit.

Next I figured that it must be a teaching of some sort. In spiritual circles, that is always the safest bet. If you don't understand something, especially something unpleasant, you assume that it is really a teaching in disguise. So you bite the bullet and rack your brain in the effort to figure out what the lesson might be.

As it turned out, there *was* a kind of lesson, but not the kind I was used to being taught. It didn't come from my teacher (who, in retrospect, probably just wanted beginners to have their initial contact with a monk). It didn't even come from within. If from anywhere, it must have come from the situation itself.

The Zendo entranceway consisted of a dimly lit, wood-paneled room about the size of a large shower stall. There were two small stools along one wall so that guests could remove their shoes before entering the temple. The door person's job was to greet each guest silently as they entered, to accept any donations, and instruct them on where to put their shoes. There was just enough room for two people to bow to one another without bumping heads.

Maybe it was the quiet, the absence of any discourse, of any instruction other than my motioning to a small sign that said "Please remove your shoes," but eventually I started to like the job. The whole experience of standing with one or two other people in that tiny room was one of intimacy. There was a simplicity, a wordless perfection to the whole arrangement that I hadn't experienced since my years with Deh Chun, and I wondered how I could have missed it before.

Sometimes people needed to engage me in conversation—"Have I come to the right place?" "Is this the Zendo?" "What do you do in here?"—but even then their questions had a simplicity and an openness that, I began to realize, was the real secret of the meditative mind. Compared to what happened inside the Zendo, with its prevailing ethos, rituals, and rules, this was the moment of truth. Perhaps it is true that life poses us a riddle, and that we must sometimes make a journey in search if its solution, but the answer is always there already, before we have taken a step.

It has now been nearly eight years since I left the Zendo, and if I close my eyes I can still see every inch of it: the Japanese rock garden, the long polished floor of the meditation hall, the candle wax I was never able to remove from one of the creases in the Buddha's robe. But when I think of being there, of what it meant to me then, and what its significance is to my life today, always I find myself in the alcove, its door propped slightly open with a brick. It is chilly. The door opens. A dark-haired woman wearing a wool coat with a fur collar steps in and bows. On her shoulders there are snowflakes. Still perfect. Still white.

One Meeting, One Life

In Japanese there is an expression, *ichigo ichie*, which is mostly associated with the tea ceremony. It means "one meeting, one life," and refers to the fact that each tea gathering is totally unique. Even if it happened again (for instance, if the same guests were in attendance), the mood, the weather, the placement of the objects in the room—something would be different. Each gathering is a once-in-a-lifetime event.

In a sense, *ichigo ichie* is the secret of the present moment, because when we are fully awake to the uniqueness of each new situation, we are fully alive. We are responding directly to something fresh and new. And so we should begin and end each meditation with the thought, "This meeting will never come again."

My Japanese Zen teacher used to say *ichigo ichie* all the time. And I have to admit that I found the whole idea very oppressive. It felt like a burden having to see each moment as unique. But whenever he said it, I would try to appreciate the moment more fully, by forcing myself to look around and take notice of details that had slipped me by: the raveled thread on a cushion, the shape and texture of a cloud, the clothes people were wearing, and the quality of the overall mood. It wasn't until years later that it occurred to me that he had never meant it as an admonition.

"One meeting, one life" is the simple truth. When we observe life carefully we find that this is how things really are. This moment will never come again. The next moment, too, will never come again. And the next. There is an endless succession of unrepeatable events. To be alive is to be with them, to be a part of them, to be unique and unrepeatable ourselves. But to do that we have to be present.

Sometimes when I have gotten too little sleep the night before and everything about the day seems more difficult, more a product of my mood, I look at the sugar maple that stands outside my study window. Like all trees, it is very still. Looking at it, I always get the impression that its experience of life is far slower and more patient than my own. Even as I watch it, however, a cloud passes and the sunlight reappears on the bark. A small woodpecker rounds the trunk into the light and taps twice, flecking away a piece of bark. After that, my mood has lifted.

One meeting, one life.

Sharing with People

Sharing the present with other people is the heart of meditation practice. As long as we only meditate alone, our practice is like one of those tiny ships built with special tools inside of a bottle. Who knows whether it is really seaworthy or not?

When we join together for a present moment meeting, we first decide how long to meet. The members may hold diverse opinions on any number of issues, but they must be in agreement on this single point. If one member is not able to meditate for longer than ten minutes at a time and all the others want to go thirty minutes, then the member who wants to meditate for ten minutes may need to bow out. This will seldom happen, however, because as I have pointed out elsewhere, how long you meditate is not the point. If you find yourself a part of a present moment group that is caught up in some ascetic notion about meditation, it is best to leave at once and find another group. The point is to come to rest in the moment and to share that experience with others as simply and as openly as possible. With that spirit in mind, it will seldom be the case that the participants cannot reach some compromise.

The second thing you need to decide is who will be responsible for watching the time. This job should rotate among all the members, even if one person doesn't mind doing it all the time. The reason is simple. The psychology of group meditation naturally invests the timekeeper with a certain authority. There is nearly always the feeling that the person keeping time is "in control." To a certain extent this is true, because during the meeting we entrust that person with the job of watching our time so we don't have to watch it for ourselves. But if the same person keeps time *all* the time, some members—including the timekeeper—may begin to get the idea that that person is an authority. This is a burden not only to the other members, but also to the timekeeper, and so we avoid this by sharing the responsibility evenly among all the members.

The meeting begins with a greeting—something simple like "Welcome." During the meeting no one talks. Everyone shares the present together in silence. Without words to spark disagreement—without ideas to draw the metes and bounds of different races, religions, classes, occupations, or beliefs—we are all together. There is nothing to agree or disagree on, there is only now. Whatever thoughts, fantasies, resentments, or bones to pick, for the moment they become our own responsibility. For the moment, they are only another thing happening inside our mind.

When the meeting is over the timekeeper says "Thank you," and immediately adds, "This meeting is over," after which everyone is free to talk or remain quiet as they please. At first, these last words may seem unnecessary, just a way of stating the obvious, but the more you meditate the more you will realize how essential they are.

In meditation, there is an enormous difference between doing it and talking about it. We experience this even during the meditation itself, when we invent a story line about meditating instead of counting the breaths from one to four. It actually takes quite some time to learn to meditate instead of just silently talking to ourselves. Matters are only made worse when we confuse discussions *about* the present moment with the present itself. That is why the timekeeper says, "This meeting is over." It tells us that now it is all right to talk, to go back to our normal pre-occupations, ideas, and beliefs; the meditation itself is done.

These are the only rules governing the present moment meeting. They are designed to help us to share the present with one another. That is all.

Sharing Yourself
with Others

When my daughter was three, we placed her in a local parents' cooperative nursery school in Woodstock. There she played and made friends with seven other children from the neighborhood three mornings a week.

One morning, as we were getting her ready to go to school, she began to look around at the last minute for something to share with the other children. She picked up a rattle belonging to her younger brother, but then discarded it. Then she selected one of her dolls, but we reminded her that she wasn't allowed to bring any of her toys to school. Finally she announced, "I'll share me." This seemed like a good idea, since it streamlined the ordeal of getting her to school on time, so we accepted her solution without further ado. "That's nice, muffin," my wife said. "You can just share *you.*"

When we dropped her off at school, however, we discovered that it had been her scheduled day to share something special with the other kids. We hadn't realized this and we were sorry we had rushed her out the door. "We ought to be helping her more with stuff like that," said my wife. "We should have remembered that it was her day to share and taken some time beforehand to help her decide what to bring." But a week later, when we attended the mid-year parent conference, we changed our minds.

As it turned out, on the day in question, as the children all sat in a circle on the floor waiting to see what Sophie had brought to share, she announced, "I'm sharing me," and let it go at that. When her teacher, Cheryl, asked her if she wanted to stand up and show the children any-thing about herself, Sophie remained seated and said, "No. I'm sharing me."

That morning the whole nursery school came to a stop. Never before had a child announced that she would just share herself and remained seated where she was, without telling a story about herself, holding onto an object, or show-ing something special that she could do. So they all sat there for a few moments, thinking about what it meant to share themselves with one another in such a simple, quiet way.

"I want to write a book about that moment," said her teacher, Cheryl. "But I wouldn't know where to begin. How do you teach that to adults?"

Like every father, I would like to think that my daugh-ter is the most gifted, most wonderful child in the world, but experience tells me that when the group spirit is right such moments just naturally occur.

It should go without saying that "I will just share me" is the right attitude to take whenever we meditate with others.

When we hold a present moment meeting, we should be ready to let go of our personal narrative—our story line about what we like, what we dislike, where we come from, and where we want to go. We ought to be ready to sit calmly for a period of time without saying anything, without attempting to explain ourselves, without saying anything *about* us, or about who we *think* we are.

I once asked a retired psychoanalyst what he thought was the most important factor in creating a successful treatment. He explained that during the first half of his career he had thought it was proper training. He had always attributed his success with clients to the fact that he had studied with so many talented analysts over the years.

"And what about now?" I asked him. "Now that you're retired?"

"Well," he explained, "now I realize that it was mostly just being able to remain open during moments of silence. Moments when nothing was being said. Thinking back on it, those were the moments when everything happened—the moments when it seemed like nothing was happening at all."

"It took thirty years to learn to let that happen," he said.

"Do you think many other analysts and psychothera-pists understand that secret?" I inquired.

"If they are successful in treating their clients, they know it," he replied. "But in most cases they don't *know* they know."

After thinking for a moment, he added, "That's the tricky thing about it, you see. It's such a simple thing."

Starting a Present Moment Group

In starting your own present moment group, there are a few practical considerations to keep in mind, such as the size of the group and the frequency and place of meeting.

As a general rule, you only need one other person to start a group—because, after all, it only takes one other person to share. But to get anything like a real group feeling, you need three or four.

With four people you could meet once a week, rotating the location of the meeting on a monthly cycle, so nobody has to play host all the time. To begin with, this is probably about ideal. You want the support of the group, and the pleasure of sharing the present with others, but not the feeling that you are being pressured to meditate more seriously or more often than you want. Meeting together once a week strikes the proper balance.

Likewise, keeping the group fairly small eliminates certain problems that groups tend to create, just by virtue of size: authority trips, for instance, or the tendency to make rules. The fewer people you have, the fewer rules you need to make. And the less tempting your group will be for people who have a strong need to control. Such people are likely to seek out larger groups, where there are more opportunities to exercise authority. As the saying goes, the best protection against theft is to own nothing. In the same way, the best protection against gurus is not having an organization to support their emotional and financial needs.

For many groups the biggest problem will be determining a place and time to meet. Given the complexity of most people's lives and the fact that we sometimes live miles apart from one another, that problem may sometimes seem impossible to solve. The key is to keep it to a very practical level, like solving a word problem in math. For instance: A, B, C, and D must all be in the same place for one hour once a week, but because A and D work from 10 to 8, B works from 8 to 5, and C works the night shift, the only available times are on the weekends, when all four want to spend time with their families. Given this situation, how can A, B, C, and D meet regularly to meditate?

The answer will vary with the individuals concerned. It may be, for instance, that the solution is for the group to meet only once a month, but for a longer period of meditation. That way they don't feel like they are losing their precious family time at home. Maybe the group splits into two parts, A with D and B with C and each group finds another member or two with similar schedules. Once people decide they want to meditate together they will find some way around obstacles of this kind.

STARTING A PRESENT MOMENT GROUP   139

A problem will come up, however, if one or more members decide that another member can't make the regularly scheduled meeting time because he or she is "not serious enough." Such an attitude defeats the whole idea of meditating as a hobby and will only create divisiveness within the group. This is the major danger of having so small a meditation group. Because then the group tends to become closely knit, and, consequently, we may become overinvested in one another's practice.

The solution to the problem is to remind ourselves that each member's meditation practice is his or her own, to practice as much or as little, as lightly or as seriously as they want. If we feel that another member is being a little too heavy-handed with us, we may sometimes need to remind that person that we are meditating because we like it, not because we ought to or because someone told us to. But we can do this in a gentle way. We all forget sometimes, and it's helpful to have other people around to remind us why we started meditating in the first place. That is one of the principal benefits of meditating in a group. The group offers the best kind of encouragement and support, which is simply meditating by your side. Preaching doesn't help, but having company does.

Don't Become an Expert

If the members of a present moment group do not assume an expert status, then when newcomers join, they will be able to have the experience of meditation for themselves. If one or all of the members assume the status of expert, however, then the experience will belong too much to them to share it with someone else. This is a kind of present moment joke, because the present belongs to everyone, not to one person or group in particular. The person who assumes that he has mastered it has forgotten what it is.

Given the natural inclination in our society to be good at something, to be productive, to know exactly what we are doing all the time, how do we avoid becoming an expert? The answer, I think, is quite simple. We just need to understand that being an expert is really a burden to us and let it go at that.

The Japanese Zen master Shunryu Suzuki said, "In the beginner's mind there are many possibilities; in the expert's, few." In essence, he meant that the more we learn, the more we are likely to become limited by what we know. This doesn't mean that meditation is anti-intellectual, or that it opposes the aims of education. It simply means that we ought not use the things we know to limit our thinking. We should use them to free our thinking instead. But, as most of us already know, to free our thinking is no easy task. Almost from birth we are told how and what to think, and gradually, as we grow older, we come to accept what we have been told as the sum total of reality. By the time we begin to meditate, most of us have thought our way inside of a box—what we think has become our world.

When we meditate we free ourselves temporarily from what we think, thereby making room for fresh possibilities, making room for something new. We accomplish this quite literally, by releasing ourselves from the hold of thought in each moment, by returning to the breath. Eventually we realize that we do not have to be a slave to our own thoughts. How many times in life have we said to ourselves, "If only for a moment I could just stop thinking." Meditation shows us how.

When we count our breaths from one to four, gradually we learn to release ourselves from thinking. Gradually, we get some sense of separation from our thoughts. This allows us a different take on ourselves. Before, we were always so identified with our thoughts that we could scarcely ever get any distance from them at all. Now, by cultivating some awareness of our own thoughts—by learning that they come and go, like breeze flowing through a room from one window to the next—we learn that thinking is there for our use and enjoyment, but not to rule our lives. Finally, it becomes possible just to be quiet for a moment and to know ourselves instead.

As I learned from Deh Chun, when you know yourself in this way, you aren't so impressed any longer by the experts. And once you are freed of that impulse—both to follow experts or to be one yourself—you aren't as likely to put obstacles in other people's way. When someone new comes to meditate with your group, you will explain as simply as possible how to meditate, and trust that if they do it themselves, they too will come to understand.

Offering Direction

As I suggested earlier in this book, the best beginning instruction in meditation is probably no instruction whatsoever but simply to sit down and be quiet. But after that first encounter, almost always something further needs to be said.

What to say and how to say it? That is the important question. Meditation is simple, but very subtle. And so, very often, words just get in the way. In my experience, there is no single set of instructions, no definitive way of presenting meditation to beginners. As long as you aren't misleading, the intent is probably a lot more important than what you say.

I think the best model for teaching meditation is to think of yourself as offering directions to the local drugstore. Everyone knows that the best directions are the simplest and most uncluttered. "Go to the end of this road and turn right. At the next traffic light take a left and look for the sign on the left that says Faye's." Very simple. Imagine how difficult it would be for someone to understand how to get to the drugstore if you began to describe all the houses along the way. What if you explained all the *wrong* ways of going to the drugstore, just in case your listener might be tempted to take one of these?

In general, the first time someone attends a present moment meeting, it should be explained to them that, ultimately, there is no method for being present. Ask them to sit still during the meditation and trust that they are present already, without doing anything at all. Explain that instructions will be offered later, but that there is no substitute for the things you can discover for yourself. Thus, the emphasis in the present moment meeting is always on self-reliance. We don't teach one another or tell one another what to do. We merely share the present. That is teaching enough.

Journey to the East

Meditation became popular in this country during the Vietnam War, when many Americans lost faith in traditional Western religious forms. The reasons for this loss of faith are extremely complex and I will not attempt to explain how factors such as expanded media coverage of the war and civil abuses by elected officials led to a deeper questioning of all traditional forms of authority. Suffice it to say that the end result was a kind of spiritual vacuum—both in the sacred and the secular realms.

To fill that void many Americans, myself included, headed East. In retrospect, I think we might have all done better just to stay put. Not that Judaism or Christianity held the answer, but because the answer was always within ourselves.

The meditative traditions of the East all point to a universal truth, one that is always discovered in the here and now. To travel East in search of it—either literally or in one's heart—only removes it that much further from our grasp. By taking a journey in search of it, we remove it by just that many miles.

How then are we to relate to meditation teachers from the various spiritual traditions of the East? Do we invest them with greater authority than our neighborhood priest, minister, or rabbi? And if so, in most cases are we not deceiving ourselves? I think the answer is to have a meditation practice of your own, one that does not rely on any external spiritual authority.

The whole notion of authority, once we examine it from a meditative point of view, is only a substitute for our own immediate experience of the here and now. To be fully present is its own authority. Only by giving that up is it possible to hand ourselves over to someone else. Only when we forget who and where we are do we need someone else to tell us. And of course, by then, things have already gone horribly wrong.

Really, we shouldn't be angry at these teachers when they tell us to just grow up and wipe our own noses. Nor should we be surprised when some of the less realized souls only want our money. That's what comes of not being present in your own life. It's like walking around wearing a placard that says, PLEASE TELL ME WHAT TO DO.

No Self-Importance

Like most people, I am sometimes guilty of remembering things differently from what they really were. Particularly in remembering Deh Chun, I sometimes have to guard myself against a kind of nostalgia about the time we spent together.

When I am honest, I will admit that I was often very uncomfortable with Deh Chun. In summer, frequently it was too hot. In winter my feet were frozen within minutes of entering the drafty little house. And then, there were the many awkward silences when I didn't have anything to say. But those momentary discomforts were nothing compared to the feeling of terror I sometimes got from being with him. Certainly not terror for my physical safety—Deh Chun was the kindest, gentlest person I have ever known. What I felt was bigger, more absolute than that: terror at the meaninglessness of life.

Deh Chun never said or did anything while I was with

him to encourage the belief that there was any point to anything other than what was there before the eye: a bowl of Chinese tea, dust motes in a shaft of morning sunlight, our shadows on the wall. There was never the sense that there was anything that one could *do* or understand. I don't mean to imply that he was in any way despairing or fatalistic about life. That would be far from the truth. Only that there was none of the usual small talk one shares with most people. None of the little shared illusions that smooth the way for so much of social intercourse, making it possible to get through life without tackling any of the big issues, like suffering or death. When I was with Deh Chun it seemed that all of the usual props that I had used to maintain a sense of self-importance were suddenly pulled away.

Deh Chun loved painting mountain landscapes with his Chinese watercolors. And he loved his small organic garden. He had friends in his neighborhood and students from the university whom he entertained lovingly. Sometimes he was invited to give a talk on Chinese landscape painting at a nearby college or museum, invitations which he accepted with some enthusiasm. But in all of these activities there appeared to be no amplification, no affectation. He simply moved from one moment to the next without self-importance of any kind.

No Rank

The present moment is not an ideology but a simple practice for ordinary men and women to follow as a part of their everyday lives. In fact, if during the practice anyone were to say "I am a Buddhist" or "I am a Christian" or "I am a follower of my guru," that thought itself would disrupt the awareness of the breath. It would substitute an idea about the self for the reality of the present place and time. Meditation is not an idea.

The philosophy of the present is to be free of ideological thinking. And this method, which does not rely upon a personal teacher or the dogma of any particular religion, favors instead the formation of small independent groups that come into being and pass easily away like wild mushrooms or grass blades in a field. It is not their aim to perpetuate themselves. Nor is their aim to acquire assets or spread their teaching. Their aim is the present, nothing more. That is the essence of what they teach.

And yet, such groups do not impinge upon the personal freedom of their members. A member may choose to study with a guru; the group may not. An individual may acquire a beautiful spot in the mountains to meditate; the group may not. The individual may be a Buddhist or a Christian. The group may not. The group may not even call itself atheist, because it is not even that. Its aim is here and now. That kind of radical poverty is its secret—the very thing that makes this form of meditation work.

But given the nature of human interactions, how do we preserve this atmosphere of openness and mutual respect? How do we preserve the spirit of "not doing" all the divisive, counterproductive things we normally do? Isn't not-doing likely to degenerate into doing instead?

The participants at a present moment gathering are without rank while they are meeting. This, really, is the essence of the present moment meeting. If that alone were preserved, then all the rest, including all the subtle aspects of the meditation itself, would naturally follow. One member might be a university president; another, a man or woman recently released from prison. Although you should not deliberately try to assemble such a diverse group, you must always remember that, at least theoretically, it is possible. And every present moment meeting should be conducted in the spirit of such a group.

At a present moment meeting there are no experts, no teachers. The person who has mastered meditation is actually the one who has *un*mastered it, the one who has given up all the various ways we have of keeping ourselves unhappy, by living in the future or the past. Even so, one isn't likely to notice. There aren't any badges or special robes for this kind of thing.

Practice

For a moment, practice taking off robes and badges, so that you can remain with the present, completely free and clear. This is the spiritual and psychological equivalent of being naked. But, while being physically naked attracts lots of attention, being spiritually naked is just the opposite. It won't attract any attention at all.

Begin by thinking about such things as your job or profession, whether or not you have lots of money, and about whatever houses and automobiles you own. Take these off, like removing an overcoat, and place them beside you on the floor. Beside these, place your clothes—your political party and/or philosophical persuasion, your religious affiliation, if any, and any books you have recently read. On top of these, pile all of your jewelry—your affectations, pretensions, all the things you project about yourself into the world. If you walk with a cane—if you suffer from tobacco, alcohol, or drug addiction, or from a painful psychological memory—toss it on the pile. Finally, remove even your underwear and socks. Think of these as your last protection against nothingness—the very things you cling to to stay alive.

What is left? And how different is it from anybody else?

Sunrise

This morning the sunrise was spectacular. Miles of it were visible through the sliding glass door of our upstairs bedroom. The kids were in bed with us: Jonah nursing, Sophie snuggled up between us, playing with her mother's hair. I don't remember her climbing into bed.

The color of the clouds was not red but incandescent orange, a color I have never seen before in nature. After getting Sophie's bottle, instead of going downstairs to meditate, I got back into bed and we all watched the sunrise until its colors were gone.

Dinner came early. Afterward we had to get the children bathed right away so that Perdita could go to her monthly parents' cooperative meeting. Tonight the topic was spiritual parenting, and everyone was present. This is Woodstock, famous for the rock concert that bore its name and an arts colony for over two hundred years, so discussions on spirituality are hardly ever a rubber-stamp affair.

One woman began by discussing her Catholic upbringing. As a young woman she had rejected it, only to come back again when she had children of her own. Another woman, a convert to Tibetan Buddhism, related the story of caring for a dying child. "It was such a gift to me," she said. A few minutes later another woman said that she had lost a child and it was not a gift. The room was silent. "It's a mystery," she said.

In all, there were Jews and Unitarians, Catholics and Buddhists, and several people who called themselves "Nothings," for the lack of a label that applied. According to Perdita, the discussion ran for three hours, at the end of which nothing had been resolved. Only, at one point, her friend Nancy said she felt that it was important for her children's spiritual development to get them out into nature every day. Everyone agreed with that. But aside from going outside every day, or maybe camping, it seemed too broad a form of spirituality to be functional in any applied sort of way.

At home Perdita told me that when people were telling everyone what religion they belonged to, she couldn't decide. Finally she told them that she practices at the Zen monastery in nearby Mt. Tremper, but that she doesn't consider herself a Buddhist. "The truth is, underneath it all, I'll probably always be more Catholic than anything else," she explained.

"What do you mean, you're not Buddhist?" said Wendy, our Tibetan Buddhist friend.

"I mean, I *practice* Zen, but I'm not a Zen *Buddhist*," she replied.

Perdita said she felt frustrated; unable to explain clearly what she meant.

Nancy, who also studies at the Zen monastery, came to her rescue. "You don't have to be Buddhist to study Zen."

All of this piqued the interest of one of the men. He'd been interested in learning how to meditate, but he was Catholic. "So where does that leave me?" he said.

"But there was one really nice thing that happened," Perdita said, at the end of recounting the night.

"What's that?" I inquired.

"Everyone saw the sunrise this morning."

"Everyone?" I said.

"Every single one."

Sharing with
Places and Things

Because we have a limited notion of what it means to share the present with others, when we meditate by ourselves, most of us don't think of it as holding a meeting. The truth is, we never meditate alone. There are always other beings with us. Animate or not, they are present too.

Once when I was living in the monastery, I was witness to something extraordinary. It happened in the summertime, during a seven-day silent retreat. After lunch each day, there was a break of about one hour, during which time many of the participants would relax in the sun on the hillside by the lake. During one break, I happened to notice my best friend, the Japanese monk Essan, standing with his arms stretched around a tree. He remained that way for a long time, with his face pressed up against the bark.

By that time tree-hugging had already become something of a cliché. "Tree hugger" was the way big business referred to people who put ecology before all other concerns.

But I did not think that this was what Essan had in mind. In fact, I wasn't at all sure *what* he had in mind. But when he continued to stand like that for the better part of an hour, I became worried and walked over to see if there was something I should do.

As I approached him, he finally seemed ready to release his hold. When he turned I could see that his face was covered with tears. I wanted to say something, but he only shook his head and smiled.

Essan was one of the most beautiful people I have ever known, but to look at him objectively, you would have had to conclude that, by ordinary standards, he was actually quite ugly. He had an enormous sloped forehead, fully visible because of his shaved head, and his upper teeth protruded from his mouth at an angle one might have politely described as "startling." But on that day his face was extraordinary. As he smiled at me I felt all my worry for him dissipate. In fact, I felt all my worry about *everything* disappear. And I remember thinking that I had seen something remarkable, though I couldn't say what it was.

A few days later the retreat was over. The guests who had joined us for the week were gone, and it was just me and Essan with the chain saw again, alone on the mountain cutting wood.

During a break, as we sat together on a log, I asked him, "So what was that about, that business with the tree?" He was quiet for a minute, then he said, "I was looking at this tree when suddenly I was overcome with love for it, so I walked up and just held it for a long time. Then, all at once, I knew. He was my brother. We were part of the same thing."

Perhaps it is easier for most of us to think of sharing the present with a plant or tree, because these things are alive. But the wind is living, too. As are dust motes and clouds, the sounds of traffic and the grainy texture of a wooden floor. All of these things share the present moment with us. The more we meditate, the broader our understanding of life is, and the more we are able to understand that the present has no borders. Everything around us is also vibrant and alive.

Practice

Close this book and hold a present moment meeting that includes everything in your immediate environment: trees, the wall clock, dripping rain. If sunlight falls through an open window onto the floor in front of you, welcome the sunlight as a member of your group. In a sense, this is the purest, most natural way of meeting, because no instruction has to be offered. And there are no rules to be obeyed. There is nothing to do and nothing to know. Therefore, there is no uncertainty or confusion.

If you now count your breaths for a few minutes, then follow the breath, after a while, almost without effort, you will begin to feel the artificial boundaries that separate human from nonhuman, animal from mineral, dissolve of their own accord.

When this happens, you will know that these other beings are always in the present. Wind blows. The leaf shadows shift their places on the floor.

Begin now.

Sharing the Present with Children

I recently attended the Sunday kid's program at a Zen monastery. One of the monastics, a kind-hearted woman wearing a black robe, was teaching the children to meditate.

"First we will begin by making our backs straight," she explained. The children all fidgeted into the required position, making their small backs perfectly rigid. The effect was slightly comical and one of the older children, a six-year-old girl who is the daughter of a friend, pursed her lips in mock seriousness and stole a glance in my direction, suppressing a laugh.

The woman continued: "Now we place our hands together, holding the left palm over the right palm in our laps, with our thumbs touching lightly."

When all the children were positioned correctly, she continued. "Now lower your eyes and look at the floor just in front of you. Putting the tip of your tongue behind your two front teeth, relax your shoulders and feel the breath coming in and going out through your nose. Just notice that, and think about how that feels."

Following this, we all meditated for a few minutes—too long for my daughter, who rose after a minute and tip-toed into the adjacent room. There, she skipped lightly in a circle with her arms extended, presumably in the effort to fly.

When the meditation was over, the woman asked all the children what it felt like to meditate. The children had various answers. "It was quiet." "It was peaceful." "I got dizzy." "I could hear the earth."

Later, one of the adult participants asked me, "So what did you think? I was amazed at how well they did."

"Yes," I said. "I think that was the problem. They were pretending to meditate, like my daughter was pretending to fly."

My brother-in-law once told me a story about Khenpo Karthar Rinpoche, a Tibetan Buddhist lama and a well-known teacher in the West. Once when he was giving a talk, one of the participants asked, "Rinpoche, how should I teach my child to meditate?"

The rinpoche looked troubled. "Oh, please don't do that," he replied.

But the man persisted. "The meditation you've taught us has been so helpful to me, Rinpoche, and I want my child to have that, too."

Again Khenpo Karthar Rinpoche said no, and again the man persisted. And so, finally he said, "If you really *must* teach your child to meditate, do it this way. Strike a bell and ask him to listen. Ask him to tell you when it stops."

This is an excellent lesson, in so many different ways. First of all, it is not necessary to teach children to meditate, any more than it is necessary to teach them how to play. Children are naturally present, without any interference or instruction on our part. Asking them to meditate only removes them from the natural state of presence in which they so often are to be found: dancing, making things, listening to rainfall on the roof, or just looking at an acorn or a fallen branch.

The house we live at in Woodstock is entirely glass at the back. Behind the house is a small field with a pond that draws all kinds of animals, from squirrels to deer to great blue herons and, occasionally, black bears. On the upstairs floor my office also looks out over this pond, but from a slightly higher vantage point, so that, during the day while I am writing, it often happens that I am the first to notice some new animal in the yard. When that happens, I call out to my daughter and immediately hear the drumming of her footsteps on the floor.

Seconds later she is standing beside me looking where I point. Her eyes stop blinking. Her breath quickens and then slows. Her pint-sized body becomes perfectly still. A minute or two later she pulls my pant leg and whispers, "Daddy, what's it called?"

Meditation
without Gurus

Not so long ago I was talking to a friend who had recently become a nun. She had a shaved head and wore the robes of a monastic. It took a while to catch up on what had happened since we last had a chance to talk. "So what kind of book are you working on?" she asked finally.

"I'm writing a book for people who want to meditate with the lives they have," I answered, "a book for people who don't want to adopt a new religion or hand all their money over to some organization. You know, meditation without gurus—something like that."

She seemed to think about this for a minute. Finally she said, "But that's what *I* wanted."

At first I thought she was kidding, but then I realized that she was not.

"So what happened?" I asked.

"I don't know," she replied.

This scenario is not at all uncommon. In fact, much the same thing happened to me.

I first started to meditate because I wanted the sense of being authentically present in my life. There was an inner knowledge, always somehow elusive, that I didn't need to *go* anywhere or *do* anything to have this authentic feeling, that I could do it right here and now, but I couldn't articulate the reasons why. I had been raised—by my parents, by my education, by the very society in which I lived—to accept nothing as certain that wasn't accompanied by a detailed explanation and to trust the opinion of experts before my own, so I assumed I must be wrong.

About that time I met Deh Chun. Deh Chun did nothing to encourage me in the belief that I ought to study meditation. In fact, he gave no explanation or instruction of any kind. At the time, I took that as an indication that he had nothing to offer, apart from the inspiring simplicity with which he lived his life. To me he seemed like something of an idiot savant, a spiritual simpleton and nothing more. Now, I realize that his was always the perfect teaching on meditation, that everything I learned thereafter was only an elaboration of what Deh Chun had taught me without ever saying a word.

Then, however, I felt that I was somehow incomplete. I couldn't shake off the feeling that I was lacking, that my impulse to act self-reliantly was merely an inbred cultural flaw, a spiritual optimism and naiveté I had only by virtue of being an American. My innate confidence in myself to experience meditation directly was only arrogance. I had better let go of it and put my faith in something else.

That self-doubt made me fair game for just about any spiritual teacher who came along. Fortunately, I found a good one, the abbot of a Zen monastery in upstate New York who was able to articulate the teachings that Deh Chun had embodied but had steadfastly refused to explain. Even so, the abbot's teaching was limited by the very explanations he used to convey it, and so finally I had to leave him and his monastery in order to experience the present moment free of all ideological constraints. Only then did I realize what Deh Chun had been trying to teach.

Sometime shortly after Deh Chun moved to Tennessee, a Theravadin Buddhist monk in New York told a young man who years later became an acquaintance of mine that if he was really serious about studying Zen he would go, not to the various temples and Zen centers that were springing up in the Northeast about that time, but to Monteagle, Tennessee. There lived an old nobody who, nevertheless, was the Real McCoy.

The young man wrote to Deh Chun on this monk's recommendation and was told that he should come to Monteagle to stay that summer. When he wrote back and asked how he would find his house, Deh Chun sent a postcard that said only, "Ask for the Chinaman." Though doubtful, he followed the old monk's instructions. He arrived by Greyhound bus in Monteagle and was shown right to Deh Chun's door.

He spent the summer living with Deh Chun, meditating with him and helping to make necessary repairs to his house, and then returned to New York. As he told me years later, he had the feeling that he had learned something wonderful, but finally inexplicable, from the old monk. Thinking that he should write and thank him, he sent a letter to Deh Chun saying how grateful he was and how much he felt he had learned from him during the time they spent together.

A week later he received a letter thanking him for all the help he had provided in fixing up the house. But at the end Deh Chun added, "Regretfully, however, I have to inform you that you learned nothing from me at all." Thirty years later, when he told me this, there was emotion in my friend's voice. When he didn't continue, I thought the story had bottomed out into some private reverie. But after a moment he added, "You know, at the time, I was so disappointed. I didn't understand what he meant at all."

For a long time I thought that Deh Chun's refusal to accept students was merely a way of insuring that he could devote all his time to meditation. He didn't want to be anyone's guru, I told myself, because he just wanted to *do* it all the time. But now I think I was wrong about that, as about so many other things concerning the enigmatic old man. Now I think he refused to be a guru because there are no gurus. There is only the present we share with everyone and everything that is. Nobody owns that. And certainly it cannot be taught. Deh Chun didn't want anyone else to trust him. He wanted them to trust themselves.

The Wooden Bowl

The day I told Deh Chun that I had decided to study with someone else, he only bowed his head. I think he may have said something under his breath, but if so, I never learned what it was. For a long time I remembered that moment with great sadness. I had been with Deh Chun since college, but without the feeling that I had ever gotten any teaching from him. Never once did he give me anything even approaching what might be called basic instruction. And when I finally *did* learn how to meditate, it wasn't from him but from the Zen master at the monastery in upstate New York.

Perhaps I had hoped that someday Deh Chun would reveal himself fully as the master that he was, but that never happened. More often, he was an embarrassment to me, an uncouth old Chinaman who blew his nose onto the sidewalk, disliked wearing his dentures, and dressed in shabby secondhand clothes.

That day, I told him I was going to formally become a student of the Japanese Zen master I had met some years before, and that I wanted someday to become a monk. I didn't say I wanted to be a Zen master, to be a part of a formal lineage of teachers that stretched in an unbroken line all the way back to the historical Buddha. I didn't tell him that I wanted to follow a "higher calling," to be the head of a monastery and train monks like I believed a real Zen master was supposed to do. Thinking back on it though, all this must have been apparent to him as we stood there together at his door.

What did it feel like to be in his shoes at that moment? To feel this tall, gangly American towering over him, so full of grim determination to realize his spiritual goal? Was he disappointed that I hadn't realized the nature of our relationship? Was he discouraged that I hadn't understood anything at all? Had it always been his purpose to let me go like that—like the man in the Buddhist parable whose friend, unbeknownst to him, had sewn a precious jewel inside the lining of his robe?

Even today I don't know the answer to any of these questions. But I have thought innumerable times about the significance of that parting gesture. At the time I thought it was simple acquiescence, the graceful acceptance of a parting that had been inevitable from the very first time we met. Years later, it seems more like the gesture of an accomplished swimmer who dives easily beneath the power of a cresting wave.

Though people who devote their lives to the fulfillment of a lofty spiritual ideal do occasionally become saints, they

never learn to meditate that way. Like the Grail of one leg-
end, meditation, when it finally comes, turns out to be
nothing but a simple wooden bowl. I began to realize that
years later as the priest at a temple in New York.

My friends were proud of me. My Japanese Zen
teacher was confident that I would continue on the path of
Zen for the rest of my life. Most people, at least within the
Zen community, treated me with some degree of deference
and respect. Even my parents, both Christians, had conced-
ed that maybe a lot of the difficulties I had experienced as
an adolescent were because it was my destiny to fulfill this
special though unusual role.

A therapist I consulted at that time disagreed. He told
me that something had gone terribly wrong with my life. I
was relieved to find someone so honest, and so after that
initial meeting, we spent several years trying to find out
what the problem might be.

By that time the monkhood seemed irrelevant, so I left
it and worked at various different jobs. Lots of answers
came out of the therapy sessions in that little room on West
57th Street, which in many ways felt like the room I'd sat in
with Deh Chun. But the only answer that stuck, the only
one that touched me deeply enough to offer anything like
guidance in my life, was the image of my teacher's bowed
head. By then its message was as plain as if the words had
been written on top of his head: If you want to be sincere,
be simple; if you want to meditate, stay low.

Printed in the USA
CPSIA information can be obtained
at www.ICGtesting.com
JSHW022345140824
68134JS00019B/1688